BBC ACTIVE

D0300793

Mandarin Chinese

talk

Yu Feixia
Alwena Lamping
Series Editor: **Alwena Lamping**

BBC Active, an imprint of Educational Publishers LLP, part of the Pearson Education Group, Edinburgh Gate, Harlow, Essex CM20 2JE, England

First published 2008.

ISBN 978-1-4066-1401-5

Cover design: adapted from original artwork by Helen Williams and Matt Bookman
Cover photograph: © Keren Su / China Span / Alamy
Insides design: Nicolle Thomas, Rob Lian
Layout: Pantek Arts Ltd. www.pantekarts.co.uk
Illustrations © Tim Marrs @ Central Illustration Agency
Publisher: Debbie Marshall
Development editor: Kan Qian
Project editor: Emma Brown
Marketing: Fiona Griffiths
Senior production controller: Franco Forgione

Audio producer: Martin Williamson, Prolingua Productions
Sound engineer: Katy Brier and Paul Kirkin at The Audio Workshop
Presenters: Sun Chen, Wang Xiaoning, Chuanzi Xing, Howard Zhang

Printed and bound in the UK by Ashford Colour Press Ltd

The Publisher's policy is to use paper manufactured from sustainable forests.

Contents

Introduction

Welcome to **Talk Mandarin Chinese**, BBC Active's new course for absolute beginners. Designed for adults, learning at home or in a class, it's the ideal introduction to Mandarin Chinese, covering the basic everyday language for a visit to China.

Talk Mandarin Chinese is suitable whether you want to learn for work or for fun, and as preparation for a first level qualification, since the course covers the Breakthrough level of the national Languages Ladder. The language is presented using *pinyin*, the official system of using roman script, i.e. the same alphabet as English, to represent the sounds of Chinese. You'll also learn to recognise some basic Chinese characters.

Talk Mandarin Chinese is an interactive course consisting of a book and two 60-minute CDs recorded by native Chinese speakers. Although designed to be used with the audio, the book could be used separately since the complete audio transcripts are included.

Talk Mandarin Chinese encourages you to make genuine progress and promotes a real sense of achievement. The key to its effectiveness lies in its systematic approach. Key features include:

- simple step-by-step presentation of new language
- involvement and interaction at every stage of the learning process
- useful language learning strategies
- regular progress checks
- reference section, including pronunciation guide, grammar summary, audio transcripts and glossary

Acknowledgements

BBC Active would like to thank everyone who contributed to this course. Our particular thanks go to Kan Qian, Dr Yu Hong Zhang, Wang Xiaoning, Li-yun Liao and Liu Chang.

> Wherever you see this: **1•5**, the phrases or dialogues are recorded on the CD (i.e. CD1, track 5).

How to use Talk Mandarin Chinese

Each of the ten units is completed in ten easy-to-follow steps.

1   Read the first page of the unit to focus on what you're aiming to learn and to set your learning in context. Then follow steps 2 to 5 for each of the next four pages.

2   Listen to the key words and phrases – don't be tempted to look at them first. Then listen to them again, this time reading the *pinyin* version in your book too. Finally, try reading them out loud before listening one more time.

3   Work your way, step by step, through the activities. These highlight key language elements and are carefully designed to develop your listening skills and your understanding of Chinese. You can check your answers in *Transcripts and answers* starting on page 99.

4   Read the **Zài Zhōngwén lǐ** explanations of how Chinese works as you come to them – they're placed just where you need that information. Some are developed further in the *Grammar* section.

5   After completing the activities, close your book and listen to the conversations straight through. The more times you listen, the more familiar Chinese will become and the more comfortable you'll become with it. You might also like to read the transcript at this stage.

6   Complete the consolidation activities on the *Put it all together* page, checking your answers with the *Transcripts and answers*.

7   Use the language you've just learnt. The audio presenters will prompt you and guide you through the *Now you're talking!* page as you practise speaking Chinese.

8   Check your progress. First, test your knowledge with the quiz. Then check whether you can do everything on the checklist – if in doubt, go back and spend some more time on the relevant section. You'll have further opportunities to check your progress in the strategic *Checkpoints* after units 4, 7 and 10.

9   Read the learning strategy at the end of the unit, which provides ideas for consolidating and extending what you've learnt.

10 Finally, relax and listen to the whole unit, understanding what the people are saying in Chinese and taking part in the conversations. This time you may not need to have the book to hand, so you can listen anywhere you choose.

Pronunciation guide

1   Most consonants sound broadly similar in *pinyin* and English, except for the following, which sound approximately like the highlighted English sounds.

c	q	x	z	zh
pa**ts**	**ch**in	**sh**in	pa**ds**	fu**dge**

2   The six basic vowel sounds are:

a	e	i	o	u	ü
art	h**er**	s**ee**	**o**re	r**u**de	French t**u**

- **i** after **c**, **ch**, **s**, **sh**, **z**, **zh** or **r** loses its basic sound and is almost swallowed up by the preceding consonant.
- **ü** after **j**, **q**, **x** and **y** is written **u** but still pronounced **ü**.
- generally, combined vowels retain their individual basic sound:

ai	a**i**sle		eng	hu**nger**
iau	mi**aou**		uo	**wo**re

But a few sound slightly different:

ang	mo**n**ster		ei	**eigh**t		en	e**n**d
iang	**you**ng		ui	**wa**y			

3   The distinctive sing-song quality of Chinese is due to its tones, of which Mandarin Chinese has four. Each different tone, indicated by a tone mark over the vowel, brings an entirely different meaning to the same combinations of letters: **yū** *silt*, **yú** *fish*, **yǔ** *rain*, **yù** *jade*

1st tone	–	high pitch, flat and steady
2nd tone	´	rising, rather like the query *Yes?*
3rd tone	ˇ	falling then rising, like **Běi** in **Běijīng**
4th tone	`	falling sharply, like **shì** in **shìchǎng**

- A syllable without a tone is pronounced without emphasis.
- An apostrophe is used to separate syllables if there's potential confusion.
- When two third tones or two fourth tones follow each other, the first is said as a second tone: **nǐ** and **hǎo** together sound like **ní hǎo**; **bù** and **shì** together sound like **bú shì**.

Nǐ hǎo

saying hello

... and goodbye

introducing yourself

... and getting to know people

Zài Zhōngguó *In China* ...

the family name, usually a single syllable such as **Wú**, **Lǐ** or **Chén**, comes before the given name. Ms **Wáng**, whose given name is **Wěiléi**, would introduce herself as **Wáng Wěiléi** (although when speaking English she might follow the English order).

The given name on its own is used among family and friends and on less formal occasions, while the full name is used more routinely than in the West. To say hello to Ms **Wáng** you'd say **Wáng Wěiléi, nǐ hǎo**. It's also common for people who know each other to use **xiǎo** *little/young* or **lǎo** *old* with the surname: someone older than **Wáng Wěiléi** could call her **Xiǎo Wáng**, whereas someone younger might use **Lǎo Wáng**.

Saying hello

1 1•2 Listen to the key language:

hǎo	good/well
Nǐ hǎo.	Hello.
Nín hǎo.	Hello. (more formal)
Nǐ/nín hǎo ma?	How are you?
(Wǒ) hěn hǎo	(I'm) very well
... xièxie. Nǐ ne?	... thank you. You?
Mǎmǎhūhū.	So-so. *Lit.* horse horse tiger tiger

Nǐ hǎo

2 1•3 Luó Píng, a receptionist at the Zhōngshān Hotel, is arriving at work. Listen and decide how she is – is she well or just so-so?

Zài Zhōngwén lǐ In Chinese ...

when you're addressing more than one person, **nǐ** *you* becomes **nǐmen**.

men can also be added to: **wǒ** *I* – **wǒmen** *we*

tā *he/she/it* – **tāmen** *they*   **G3**

3 1•4 Now listen as Luó Píng greets various guests and colleagues at the hotel.

- Does she greet one person or a couple first?
- How many times do you hear **xièxie** *thank you*?

4 1•5 **Hǎo** is also part of **zǎoshang hǎo** *good morning* and **wǎnshang hǎo** *good evening*. During the day, Luó Píng greets the following people. Listen and tick which greeting she uses.

	nǐ hǎo	zǎoshang hǎo	wǎnshang hǎo
Fàn Yǒng			
Wú Lán			
Lǐ xiānsheng *Mr Li*			
Wáng Yáunyuan			
Chén Jiàntāo			

... and goodbye

5 **1•6** Listen to the key language:

Zàijiàn

Zàijiàn.	Goodbye. *Lit*. Again see.
Huítóu jiàn.	See you later.
Wǎnshang jiàn.	See you this evening.
Míngtiān jiàn.	See you tomorrow.
Wǎn'ān.	Goodnight. *Lit*. Evening peace.

6 **1•7** Listen to Fàn Yǒng saying goodbye to the following people at the Zhōngshān Hotel, and match them with the above phrases.

Lǐ xiānsheng	**Zhào Mǐn**	**Chén tàitai** *Mrs Chén*
Lǐ Yǒng	**Zhào Wěiléi**	

7 **1•8** Students Tíngting, Léilei and Han leave the lobby next. Listen and jot down in pinyin and English when Han expects to see the others next.

Shénme shíhòu? *When?*

Tíngting .... **Léilei** ....

8 **1•9** You might find it helpful at this point to read about tones on page 6. Then listen to the five ways of saying **ma**, which have entirely different meanings:

mā *mother* **má** *linen* **mǎ** *horse* **mà** *swear* **ma** *question word*

Now listen and decide which words you hear from these sets.

bái *white*		**bǎi** *hundred*	
é *goose*		**è** *hungry*	
sī *silk*		**sì** *four*	
wō *nest*		**wǒ** *I*	
wū *house*		**wǔ** *five*	
yú *fish*		**yù** *jade*	

Finally, listen and put the correct tone accent on these words.

cha *tea* **che** *car* **bei** *north* **xi** *west* **wo** *lie* **lu** *road* **yu** *rain*

Introducing yourself

1 **1•10** Listen to the key language:

Duìbuqǐ.	Excuse me.
Wǒ shì ...	I'm ...
Wǒ bú shì ...	I'm not ...
Nǐ shì ... ma?	Are you ...?
Nín shì Chén xiānsheng ma?	Are you Mr Chén?
shì, shìde/bú shì	yes/no

2 **1•11** Luó Píng has a message for a Mr Chén. Listen as she tries to find him in the busy hotel lobby, and tick off the key phrases you hear listed above.

Zài Zhōngwén lǐ In Chinese ...

to make a statement into a question, you just add **ma**:

Tā shì Chén xiānsheng.	He's Mr Chén.
Tā shì Chén xiānsheng ma?	Is he Mr Chén?

---

3 **1•12** Listen to someone else checking in at the Zhōngshān Hotel, focus on his name, and decide which of these names is his.

a **Gāo Zhìqiáng**   b **Gāo Zǐxiáng**   c **Gāo Zìxiáng**

Zài Zhōngguó In China ...

a man can be addressed as **xiānsheng**, a woman as **nǚshì** and a younger woman as **xiǎojie**. Or, if you know a woman's married, you can address her as **tàitai**. These words are also used as titles after the name: **Gāo Míng xiānsheng** *Mr Gāo Míng*; **Huáng Mèngjié nǚshì** *Ms Huáng Mèngjié*. You never use a title when giving your own name.

---

4 How would you

a ask a young woman if she's Miss Zhōng,
b reply if someone asked you that question,
c say who you are?

... and getting to know people

5 **1•14** Listen to the key language:

Nǐ xìng shénme?	What's your surname?
Wǒ xìng ...	My surname is ...
Nǐ jiào shénme?	What's your name?
Wǒ jiào ...	My (full) name's ...
Hěn gāoxìng rènshi nǐ.	Very pleased to meet you.

6 **1•15** Listen to Zhào Zhōuzhou saying what her name is when she meets a new colleague. Does she use **Wǒ xìng** or **Wǒ jiào?**

7 **1•16** Zhào Zhōuzhōu works on the front desk of a large recruitment company. Listen as she welcomes somebody, and pick out the visitor's names from the following. You might like to refer to page 6 first.

Surname	**Wáng**	**Huáng**	**Hóng**
Given name	**Xuě**	**Qiáng**	**Shēng**

Zài Zhōngwén lǐ In Chinese ...

question words such as *who? what? where?* go in the same position as the answer.

Tā jiào <u>shénme</u>?	*What's his/her name? Lit. He/She called what?*
Tā jiào <u>Lǐ Xiǎoyuè</u>.	*Her name's Li Xiǎoyuè.* **G10**

---

8 **1•17** Lǐ Xiǎoyuè has arranged to meet someone at the recruitment office. He's older and of a higher social status, so she uses **nín** to convey respect. Listen and complete the conversation, including the tone accents.

- .... hǎo. .... shì Wáng Hǎiqìng xiānsheng ....?
- Shì, ... shì.
- Wǒ .... Lǐ Xiǎoyuè. .... gāoxìng rènshi ....

put it all together

1   Match the Chinese with the English. There's one phrase left over – what does it mean?

a	What's your name?	1	**Hěn gāoxìng rènshi nǐ.**
b	Hello.	2	**Wó hěn hǎo, xièxie.**
c	My name is ...	3	**Nǐ jiào shénme?**
d	Excuse me.	4	**Nǐ hǎo ma?**
e	Good evening.	5	**Duìbuqǐ.**
f	No, I'm not.	6	**Wǎnshang hǎo.**
g	Goodnight.	7	**Nǐ hǎo.**
h	I'm very well, thank you.	8	**Wǒ jiào ...**
i	Very pleased to meet you.	9	**Wǎn'ān.**
		10	**Wǒ bú shì.**

2   What could these people be saying to each other?

1

2

3

4

3   1•18 Here are some Chinese names and words you may find familiar. Try saying them out loud, concentrating on the tones, then listen to the audio to check your pronunciation.

Běijīng	Shànghǎi	Sìchuān	Xī'ān
Máo Zédōng	Hú Jǐntāo		Dèng Xiǎopíng
fēngshuǐ	gōngfu	tàijí	májiàng

now you're talking!

> **Nǐ hǎo ma?**

> **Mǎmǎhūhū.**

1   1•19 Answer as if you were Jake Newman, on holiday in
    Guangzhou and waiting to go on a tour one morning.

- Say hello to the tour rep.
- ◆ **Zǎoshang hǎo. Nǐ xìng shénme?**
- Give her the information she wants.
- ◆ **Shì Jake Newman xiānsheng ma?**
- Say yes, you're Jake Newman.

- You think you see a famous Chinese actress. Ask the rep if
  that's **Gǒng Lì.**
- ◆ **Shìde, tā shì Gǒng Lì.**

2   1•20 On the coach, the person sitting next to you starts a
    conversation.

- **Zǎoshang hǎo. Wǒ shì Huáng Nà. Nǐ jiào shénme?**
- ◆ Answer her question.
- **Hěn gāoxìng rènshi nǐ.**
- ◆ Say you're pleased to meet her.

When the tour's over you both return to your hotels, having
signed up for another tour the next day.

- Say goodbye to Huáng Nà.
- ◆ **Míngtiān jiàn.**

3   1•21 That evening, you meet a friend, Gāo Wénpíng, in the
    bar.

- Greet him.
- ◆ **Wǎnshang hǎo.**
- Ask him how he is.
- ◆ **Mǎmǎhūhū. Nǐ ne?**
- Say you're very well, thanks.

quiz

1 When would you use **nǐmen hǎo** instead of **nǐ hǎo?**

2 How might you reply to **nǐ hǎo ma?**

3 What's the difference between **wǎnshang hǎo** and **wǎnshang jiàn**? Can you work out what **míngtiān wǎnshang** means?

4 If someone asks **Tā jiào shénme?**, what do they want to know?

5 When do you say **Hěn gāoxìng rènshi nǐ?**

6 What are the words for *yes* and *no* in reply to *Are you …?*

7 Who would you address as **tàitai?**

8 Given that (*on*) *Saturday* is **xīngqīliù**, how do you say *See you on Saturday?*

Now check whether you can …

- say hello to one person or several people
- say good morning and good evening
- address someone as Mr/Ms/Mrs …
- ask someone how they are
- reply when someone asks you how you are
- introduce yourself
- reply when someone's introduced to you
- ask someone's name and give your name
- say goodbye

The best way of developing good Chinese pronunciation is by listening to the audio as often as you can and repeating things – out loud – over and over, imitating the speakers closely. It really does make a difference since it familiarises you with the sounds of Chinese and gets you used to the tones, which most people find daunting when they first start learning.

Nǐ shì nǎ guó rén?

talking about nationality

... and where you come from

saying what you do for a living

giving your phone number

Zài Zhōngguó ...

people are delighted to hear visitors speaking their language, and it's worth learning to say a little about yourself and to ask and answer simple questions so that you can make conversation with the people you meet.

When talking about where people are from, the key words are **guó** *country* and **rén** *person*. When you ask what nationality someone is – **Nǐ shì nǎ guó rén?** – literally you're asking *You are which country person?* **Rén** is tacked on to the country for the reply: **Yīngguó** *UK*, **Yīngguórén** *British*; **Měiguó** *USA*, **Měiguórén** *American*. It's not only used with countries: **Běijīngrén** *from Beijing*; **Xiānggǎngrén** *from Hong Kong*.

Talking about nationality

1 1•22 Listen to the key language:

Nǐ shì nǎ guó rén?	What nationality are you?
Wǒ shì Měiguórén.	I'm American.
Nǐ shì Yīngguórén ma?	Are you British?
Shì(de), wǒ shì Yīngguórén.	Yes, I'm British.
Bù, wǒ bú shì Yīngguórén.	No, I'm not British.

2 1•23 Wang Lan, doing some market research for a holiday company, talks to a group of tourists in Beijing. Listen and tick their nationality.

	Yīngguórén	Měiguórén	Xīnxīlánrén *from New Zealand*	Jiānádàrén *Canadian*
Tourist 1				
Tourist 2				
Tourist 3				
Tourist 4				
Tourist 5				

3 1•24 Match these **guójí** *nationalities* to the **guójiā** *countries*. Try saying them out loud, then listen, focusing on the pronunciation.

Wēi'ěrshìrén	**Àodàlìyàrén**	**Sūgélánrén**	**Yīnggélánrén**
Rìběnrén	**Ài'ěrlánrén**	**Hánguórén**	**Zhōngguórén**

guójiā		**guójí**
Zhōngguó	*China*	....
Hánguó	*Korea*	....
Rìběn	*Japan*	....
Yīnggélán	*England*	....
Sūgélán	*Scotland*	....
Wēi'ěrshì	*Wales*	....
Ài'ěrlán	*Ireland*	....
Àodàlìyà	*Australia*	....

4 How would *you* reply if someone asked **Nǐ shì Yīnggélánrén ma?**

... and where you come from

5   **1•25** Listen to the key language:

Nǐ cóng nǎr lái?	Where are you from? *Lit*. You from where come?
Wǒ cóng ... lái.	I come from ... *Lit*. I from ... come.
Nǐ shì běndìrén ma?	Are you from round here? *Lit*. You are local?
Wǒ shì Shànghǎirén.	I'm from Shanghai.
Nǐ <u>yě</u> shì Shànghǎirén ma?	Are you <u>also</u> from Shanghai?
Shì, wó yě shì Shànghǎirén.	Yes, I'm also from Shanghai.

6   **1•26** An international group of **xuésheng** *students* are asked by tutors Zhang Li and Zhou Li where they're from. Read the replies, guessing new words or checking them in the glossary, then listen and number them in the order you hear them.

- **Shìde, wǒ shì Shànghǎirén.**
- **Wǒ cóng Měiguó lái, cóng Niǔyuē lái.**
- **Bú shì, wǒ cóng Lúndūn lái.**
- **Wǒ shì Àodàlìyàrén, wǒ cóng Xīní lái.**
- **Wǒ cóng Ài'ěrlán lái.**
- **Bù. Wǒ shì Nánjīngrén ... wǒ cóng Nánjīng lái.**

Zài Zhōngwén lǐ ...

like all verbs, **shì** *to be* stays the same regardless of who's talking or being talked about:

    wǒ shì *I am*, **wǒmen shì** *we are*

    nǐ shì, **nǐmen shì** *you are*

    tā shì *he/she/it is*, **tāmen shì** *they are*

Adding **bù** makes it negative:

    nǐ bú shì *you're not*, **tāmen bú shì** *they're not*.

In reply to a question containing **shì**, *no* is **bú shì**; *yes* is **shì**, or **shìde** which is slightly more emphatic: *Yes, I am*.   **G9**

---

7   **1•27** The following place names are written as they're pronounced in Chinese. Work out what they are, then listen as Hannah, Susie and Mark say where they come from and tick the right answer.

Hannah	**Lánkǎisītè**	**Lúndūn**
Susie and Mark	**Jiālǐfúníyà**	**Kānpéilā**

Saying what you do for a living

1   **1•28** Listen to the key language:

Nǐ zuò shénme gōngzuò?	What do you do? *Lit.* You do what work?
Wǒ shì yīshēng/xuésheng.	I'm a doctor/student.
Nǐ yě shì xuésheng ma?	Are you a student too?
Wǒ xué Yīngwén.	I study English.
Wǒ zài yīyuàn gōngzuò.	I work in a hospital. *Lit.* I in hospital work.

2   **1•29** Listen to the people being interviewed about what they do, and number each person's occupation below as you hear it mentioned.

 ....
kuàijìshī

 ....
yīshēng

 ....
dǎoyóu

 ....
lǎoshī

 ....
gōngchéngshī

 ....
fúwùyuán

....
lǜshī

 ....
jìzhě

Zài Zhōngwén lǐ...

word order is very similar to English: subject + verb + object:

Wǒ jiāo Yīngwén. *I teach English.*

However, phrases referring to place or time go before the verb:

Wǒ <u>zài dàxué</u> jiāo Yīngwén. *I teach English <u>at the university</u>.*

Wǒ <u>xīngqīwǔ</u> jiāo Yīngwén. *I teach English <u>on Friday</u>.*   **G1**

---

3   **1•30** At a conference, Zhao Li is briefing a visitor. Listen several times and figure out what people do and where they work.

Bāo Yúntiān ....

Liú Chàng ....

Cài Xuán ....

Lín Jiājia ....

dàxué *university*
yīyuàn *hospital*
yínháng *bank*
gōngchǎng *factory*
gōngsī *company*
bàngōngshì *office*

Giving your phone number

1 **1•31** Listen to the numbers 0 to 10 and practise saying them aloud.

零	一	二	三	四	五	六	七	八	九	十
líng	yī	èr	sān	sì	wǔ	liù	qī	bā	jiǔ	shí
0	1	2	3	4	5	6	7	8	9	10

Zài Zhōngguó …

Arabic numbers are widely used in everyday life. People believe that 8 is very lucky and 4 is unlucky. Many go to great lengths to have a phone number or car registration with 8s, and to avoid one with 4s.

---

2 **1•32** Listen and jot down the numbers you hear.

....

3 **1•33** Now listen to these phrases relating to **diànhuà hàomǎ** *phone number*.

Nǐde diànhuà hàomǎ **shì shénme?**   What's <u>your</u> phone number?
Wǒde shǒujī hàomǎ shì…   <u>My</u> mobile number is …
Gōngsī de diànhuà hàomǎ shì …   The <u>company's</u> phone number is …

4 **1•34** Cài Xuán asks a colleague for her phone number. Try saying her mobile number before you listen, then make a note of her home **jiā** and work numbers. In lists of numbers, 1 is pronounced **yāo**, not **yī**, to avoid confusion with **qī** 7.

Wǒde shǒujī hàomǎ shì 07726 088 098
Wǒ jiā de diànhuà hàomǎ shì …………………
Wǒ gōngsī de diànhuà hàomǎ shì …………………

Zài Zhōngwén li …

de shows possession. It equates to *'s* or *of* in English: **Xuán de** *Xuán's*, **gōngsī de** *the company's*. It is also used with **wǒ, nǐ, tā** etc.: **wǒde** *my*, **nǐde** *your*, **tāmende** *their*. **De** is often omitted when referring to close personal connections: **wǒ māma** *my mother*, **wǒ jiā** *my home*, **nǐ lǎoshī** *your teacher*, **tā tóngshì** *his/her colleague*.   **G4**

---

put it **all together**

1   Which answer best fits the question?

a	Nǐ shì Yīnggélánrén ma?	1	Bú shì, wǒ shì jìzhě.
b	Nǐ shì Měiguórén ma?	2	Wǒ shì gōngchéngshī.
c	Nǐde diànhuà hàomǎ shì shénme?	3	Wǒ cóng Sūgélán lái.
d	Nǐ zuò shénme gōngzuò?	4	Bù, wǒ shì Sūgélánrén.
e	Nǐ yě shì lǎoshī ma?	5	Shì qī bā sān wǔ bā jiǔ.
f	Nǐ cóng nǎr lái?	6	Shì, wǒ shì Měiguórén.

2   Yú Jiànzhōng is a doctor from Beijing, and his clinic's telephone number is **líng yāo líng bā wǔ wǔ líng jiǔ yāo liù liù**. How would he complete this form in pinyin? **Zhíyè** is *occupation*.

xìng ....   guójí ....

zhíyè ....   diànhuà hàomǎ ....

3   Complete this description of Liáng Hǎijiāo from Guǎngzhōu with appropriate words from the box. She's a lawyer, working for a bank.

cóng   yínháng   lǜshī
jiào   xìng   lái

Wǒ .... Liáng. Wǒ .... Liáng Hǎijiāo.
Wǒ shì Guǎngzhōurén, wǒ ....
Guǎngzhōu .... Wǒ zài ....
gōngzuò, wǒ shì ....

4   Using 3 as a guide, write down how these people might describe themselves.

Huáng Méilíng   Rhodri Daniels
Accountant, works in office   Teacher in university
Chinese, from Hong Kong   Welsh, from Bangor

now you're talking!

1   **1•35** Take the part of Hannah Pearson in a conversation by answering the questions below, using the information from the business card.

- Pí'ěrsūn xiǎojie, nǐ shì Měiguórén ma?
- Nǐ cóng nǎr lái?
- Nǐ zuò shénme gōngzuò?

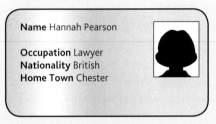

Name Hannah Pearson

Occupation Lawyer
Nationality British
Home Town Chester

2   **1•36** When on holiday in Xi'an, someone asks you where the university is – and it leads to a conversation.

- Duìbuqǐ, dàxué zài nǎr?
- Tell her you're not from the area.
- Nǐ shì Jiānádàrén ma? Yīngguórén? Měiguórén?
- Say you're British, and find out where she's from.
- Wǒ shì Yìdàlìrén.
- She's Italian. Ask if she's a student.
- Bù, wǒ jiāo Yìdàlìwén. Nǐ ne?
- Tell her you're a teacher too.
- Wǒ jiào Elena Chéng. Nǐ ne?
- Tell her your own name. Now say you're pleased to meet her.
- Wó yě hěn gāoxìng rènshi nǐ.

quiz

1 If someone tells you he's **Xiānggǎngrén**, where's he from?

2 Provide the numbers missing from this sequence: **sì ... bā ...**

3 Would **sān bā wǔ jiǔ bā** or **sān sì wǔ èr sì** be the more popular phone number in China?

4 What information do you give if you're asked **nǐde diànhuà hàomǎ shì shénme?**

5 What do you add to **Wáng xiānsheng** to mean *Mr Wáng's*?

6 On a form, what does **zhíyè** mean?

7 Can you find three pairs from the following: **gōngchéngshī, dǎoyóu, xuésheng, yīshēng, dàxué, gōngchǎng, yīyuàn.** What does the remaining word mean?

8 If **Fǎguó** is *France* and **Déguó** is *Germany*, what's the Chinese for French and German nationalities?

Now check whether you can ...

- say what nationality you are
- say where you come from
- say what you do for a living
- ask others for the above information
- use the numbers 0–10
- give your phone number

Take every opportunity to practise your Chinese: say out loud every number you see; say your **diànhuà hàomǎ** and also the numbers of friends and family; practise introducing yourself and giving your **gōngzuò** and **guójí**. To help you remember new words you could try listing them in a book, putting them on sticky labels in places where you can't fail to notice them or even recording them and comparing your pronunciation with the audio.

Zhè shì wǒ péngyou

introducing friends and colleagues

... and family

saying how old you are

talking about your family

Zài Zhōngguó ...

people are very specific when talking about family relationships.
For example, there are different words for grandparents depending on
whose side of the family they're on: **yéye** and **nǎinai** *paternal grandfather/
grandmother*, **wàigōng** and **wàipó** *maternal grandfather/grandmother*.
And when talking about siblings, the words themselves indicate position in
the family: a brother is **gēge** if he's older and **dìdi** if he's younger; a sister
is **jiějie** if she's older and **mèimei** if she's younger. These words are often
used instead of the given name.

Professional status is reflected in how you address people, with titles such
as **jīnglǐ** *manager*, **zhǔrèn** *director*, **zhǔxí** *chairman*, and **lǎoshī** *teacher* used
routinely after the surname or full name.

Introducing friends and colleagues

1 **1•37** Listen to the key language:

Zhè shì wǒ(de)	This is my
... péngyou.	... friend.
... nǚ péngyou.	... girlfriend.
... nán péngyou.	... boyfriend.
... tóngshì.	... colleague.

2 **1•38** David Rees is working in China. Listen as Wáng Lán introduces him to Liáng Xiǎoxiá, and work out

a who Liáng Xiǎoxiá is in relation to Wáng Lán,
b what her professional role is.

Listen again and complete what David says as he hands her his **míngpiàn** *business card*.

● **Wǒ .... David. .... shì .... míngpiàn.**

3 **1•39** Later, Wáng Lán takes David into town to meet various people. You'll hear **Gěi nǐ jièshào ...** *Let me introduce you to* ...

Listen then choose the correct options.

Jiǎng Yuányuan shì Wáng Lán de   tóngshì

                                         nǚ péngyou

                                         mèimei

Huáng Jiànhuán hé Xǔ Qīng shì Wáng Lán de   tóngshì

                                                    péngyou

What does David say when introduced to Huáng Jiànhuán and Xǔ Qīng?

> **Zài Zhōngwén lǐ ...**
>
> nouns don't add -s or change in any other way in the plural.
> **Péngyou** can mean *friend* or *friends* – it's up to the context to make it clear which it is.
>
> G2

.... and family

4   **1•40** Listen to the key language:

Nà shì wǒ(de)	That is my
... jiā.	... family/home.
... zhàngfu/àiren.	... husband.
... tàitai/àiren.	... wife.
... érzi.	... son.
... nǚ'ér.	... daughter.
... bàba hé māma.	... mother and father.

Zài Zhōngguó ...

àiren, meaning *loved one*, is rather like *spouse* in English, and is widely used instead of the words for husband and wife.

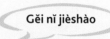

Gěi nǐ jièshào

5   **1•41** Later, David Rees meets up with his sister Jessica, a student. At her hotel they meet Xǔ Qīng and her husband. After listening to the introductions, choose the right options.

Jessica is	☐ younger	☐ older than David
Xǔ Qīng's husband is	☐ Lǎo Dèng	☐ Lǎo Zhèng
They're from	☐ Xiānggǎng	☐ Guǎngzhōu

6   **1•42** Xǔ Qīng shows Jessica and David **tāmen jiā de zhàopiàn** *their family photo*. Remind yourself of the words on page 23, listen, then jot down in Pinyin and English which members of the family are in the photo.

Saying how old you are

1   1•43 Numbers over 10 follow a very logical pattern. Listen to some of these:

11	shíyī	21	èrshíyī	40	sìshí
12	shí'èr	22	èrshí'èr	50	wǔshí
13	shísān	23	èrshísān	60	liùshí
14	shísì	24	èrshísì	70	qīshí
15	shíwǔ	25	èrshíwǔ	80	bāshí
16	shíliù	26	èrshíliù	90	jiǔshí
17	shíqī	27	èrshíqī	100	yī bǎi
18	shíbā	28	èrshíbā		31 to 99 follow the same pattern
19	shíjiǔ	29	èrshíjiǔ		as 21 to 29: **sānshíyī**, **sānshí'èr**,
20	èrshí	30	sānshí		**sānshísān**, etc.

2   1•44 You're going to hear all but one of the following numbers. Which one is it?

4   5   10   14   40   69   80   96

3   1•45 Say the following numbers out loud:

13   15   39   48   18   24

Then listen to them to see how you did.

4   1•46 Listen to the key language:

Nǐ jǐ suì le?	How old are you? (to young children)
Nǐ duō dà le?	How old are you? (to teenagers or adults)
Nǐ duō dà suìshu le?	How old are you? (to elderly people)
Wǒ/Tā 17 suì.	I am/She is/He is 17.

5   1•47 In China it's quite usual to ask personal questions when you first meet someone. Listen to various members of an extended family being asked how old they are, and make a note of their ages.

……. ……. ……. …….

Talking about your family

6 **1•48** Listen to the key language:

Nǐ jiéhūn le ma?	Are you married?
Wǒ jiéhūn le.	I'm married.
Wǒ líhūn le.	I'm divorced.
Wǒ dānshēn.	I'm single.
Nǐ yǒu háizi ma?	Do you have children?
Wǒ yǒu yī ge érzi	I have a/one son
... hé liǎng ge nǚ'ér.	... and two daughters.
Wǒ méi yǒu háizi.	I don't have children.

Zài Zhōngwén lǐ ...

you don't put a noun straight after a number, e.g. one child, two cars. There has to be a measure word (MW) between them, chosen according to what you're talking about. With people, the MW is ge: *yī ge péngyou* one friend, *sān ge lǎoshī* three teachers.

When you're talking about two of something, liǎng is used instead of èr: *liǎng ge péngyou* two friends, *liǎng ge lǎoshī* two teachers. **G8**

7 **1•49** Iwan Jones, in China on a tour, is practising his Chinese on two people he's met, Xiè Zhèngkǎi and Zhōng Jiéníng. Listen to their conversation, and work out whether they're married or not.

8 **1•49** Now listen again, this time noting what they say about their families.

	érzi	nǚ'ér
Zhōng Jiéníng		
Xiè Zhèngkǎi		
Iwan Jones		

put it all together

1   Choose the right meaning from the list in the box.

   a **yī ge érzi**
   b **liǎng ge mèimei**
   c **liǎng ge nǚ'ér**
   d **shí'èr ge péngyou**
   e **yī ge gēge**
   f **liǎng ge jiějie**

   1 older brother, 1 younger brother,1 son, 2 younger sisters,
   2 older sisters, 2 daughters, 2 sons, 2 older brothers,
   10 friends, 11 friends, 12 friends

2   Say the following numbers in Chinese then add the pairs up
   and say the answers too.

   14 + 36   21 + 22   45 + 54
   12 + 68   81 + 19   77 + 11

3   This is Xiǎoqīng's family tree.

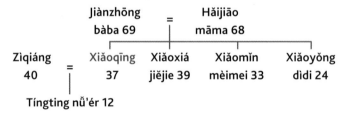

   Jiànzhōng   =   Hǎijiāo
   bàba 69   māma 68

   Zìqiáng   =   Xiǎoqīng   Xiǎoxiá   Xiǎomǐn   Xiǎoyǒng
   40   37   jiějie 39 mèimei 33 dìdi 24

   Tíngtíng nǚ'ér 12

   Choose the correct option.

   a Jiànzhōng hé Hǎijiāo   méi yǒu háizi   yǒu sì ge háizi
   b Xiǎoqīng yǒu   liǎng ge jiějie   yī ge jiějie
   c Xiǎoqīng de dìdi   jiéhūn le   dānshēn
   d Xiǎoqīng yǒu yī ge   nǚ'ér   érzi
   e Zìqiáng de àiren jiào   Tíngtíng   Xiǎoqīng

1   **1•50** You're chatting to someone in your hotel and she shows you some photos she's just taken.

- Point to a picture and ask if that's her husband.
- ◆ **Shìde, nà shì wǒde zhàngfu.**
- Now ask if this is her daughter.
- ◆ **Shìde, zhè shì wǒ nǚ'ér.**
- She seems about ten or so. Ask how old she is.
- ◆ **Tā shíyī suì.**
- Tell your English-speaking companion how old the daughter is.

2   **1•51** Read these questions, and answer them when prompted as if you were Steve, married to Olga, with two children Jack (8) and Maya (6). They're from Exeter in the UK.

- **Nǐ hǎo. Nǐ jiào shénme?**

- **Nǐ cóng nǎr lái?**

- **Nǐ jiéhūn le ma?**

- **Nǐ tàitai jiào shénme?**

- **Nǐmen yǒu háizi ma?**

- **Nǐ érzi jǐ suì le?**

- **Nǐ nǚ'ér ne?**

quiz

1 Who is a **dìdi**?

2 If you're told **Zhěngyíng sìshísì suì**, is Zhengying 14, 40 or 44?

3 What's the sum in Chinese of **shí'èr** and **liùshíqī**?

4 What word has to go between **sān** and **péngyou** to say *three friends*?

5 To say you have two children, what goes in the gaps? **Wǒ yǒu** .... **ge** ....

6 Would you say **nǐ jǐ suì le** or **nǐ duō dà le**? to ask someone in their twenties how old they are?

7 Starting with the youngest, arrange these in order of age: **wǒ wàipó, wǒ nǚ'ér, wǒ tàitai, wǒ māma.**

8 How would you introduce Zhōng Wěi, a company director?

Now check whether you can ...

- introduce friends or colleagues
- say whether you're married or not
- say if you have children
- introduce a member of your family
- use the numbers between 11 to 100
- give your age
- ask how old people of various generations are

A good way to practise talking about your family is to find a **zhàopiàn** *photograph* with lots of them on it – a wedding group is ideal. Point to each person and say their name, who they are in relation to you and how old they are. You might be able to say what some of them do for a living; and if there are different nationalities involved, you could mention that too.

Wǒ yào yī bēi lǜ chá

ordering tea and coffee

... and other drinks

offering someone a drink

making choices

Zài Zhōngguó ...

chá *tea* is a central element of the culture. Whether it's **lǜ chá** *green tea*, **hóng chá** *black (Lit. red) tea*, **wūlóng chá** *oolong tea*, **huā chá** *jasmine tea*, **júhuā chá** *chrysanthemum tea*, or one of the many other varieties available, tea is a symbol of hospitality and respect, drunk on formal and informal occasions. It's believed that each kind of tea has distinctive health-enhancing properties, with green tea being the most beneficial. **Chá** is normally served hot, without milk or sugar, although **nǎi chá** *tea with milk* and **bīng hóng chá** *iced black tea* are increasing in popularity among the younger generation.

Ordering tea and coffee

1   1•52 Listen to the key language:

Nín yào (hē) shénme?   What would you like (to drink)?
Wǒ yào   I'd like, *Lit*. I want
... yī bēi chá/kāfēi.   ... one (cup of) tea/coffee.
... yī bēi lǜ chá.   ... one (cup of) green tea.
Gěi nín/nǐmen.   Here you are. *Lit*. Give you
Xièxie. – Bú xiè/Bú kèqi.   Thank you. – You're welcome.

Zài Zhōngwén lǐ ...

if you ask for <u>a</u> tea or <u>one</u> coffee, you need to include the measure word (MW) **bēi** *cup, bowl* or *glass*: **yī bēi chá** *a/one tea*, **liǎng bēi lǜ chá** *two green teas*, **sān bēi kāfēi** *three coffees*.

---

2   1•53 Listen to various people ordering drinks in a snack bar then complete the conversation. What does the person saying **wǒmen yào** order?

- .... bēi chá.
- Wǒ yào sān .... kāfēi.
- Wǒmen ...... liǎng bēi ....
- Gěi nǐmen.
- Xièxie.
- ....

> **Nímen yào shénme?**

3   1•54 Now listen to Lín Guóqiáng and his girlfriend Zhào Měilì ordering tea. Which do they choose?

	绿茶 **lǜ chá** *green tea*	花茶 **huā chá** *jasmine tea*	红茶 **hóng chá** *black tea*
Lín Guóqiáng			
Zhào Měilì			

... and other drinks

4   **1•55** Listen to the key language:

yī guàn píjiǔ	one can of beer
liǎng guàn píjiǔ	two cans of beer
yī píng pútáojiǔ	one bottle of wine
liǎng píng júzi zhī/kělè	two bottles of orange juice/cola
sān píng (kuàngquán) shuǐ	three bottles of (mineral) water

> **Zài Zhōngwén lǐ ...**
>
> the measure word for something in a can or a tin is **guàn**, and a bottle **píng**. If ever you forget which measure word to use, you can get away with using **ge** without the noun: **Wǒ yào sān guàn píjiǔ** *I'd like three beers* or **Wǒ yào sān ge** *I'd like three (of them)*.

5   **1•56** Listen to Wáng Guānxiù ordering beer and cola in a **jiǔbā** *bar* and note how many of each he wants.

啤酒	可乐
.... **píjiǔ**	.... **kělè**

6   **1•57** The **jiǔbā** is busy. Listen as the waiter takes a drinks order for a party and make a note of what people ask for.

7   How would you order the following?

2 cups of tea
1 glass of water
1 bottle of mineral water
5 cans of cola
6 glasses of beer
1 bottle of wine
4 glasses of orange juice

Offering someone a drink

1   1•58 Listen to the key language:

Qǐng jìn/zuò.	Please come in/sit down.
Qǐng hē chá.	Please have some tea.
Wǒ hē hóng chá.	I'll have black tea.
Nǐ yào jiā niúnǎi ma?	Would you like it with milk?
Nǐ yào jiā táng ma?	Would you like it with sugar?
Hǎo, xièxie./Bú yào, xièxie.	Yes, please./No, thank you.
Zhè ge chá hěn hǎohē.	This tea is delicious.

2   1•59 Lǐ Wěi welcomes Zhāng Méi and Jon Riley, an American colleague, to his office. Listen and decide what sort of tea they both have and whether either of them takes milk and sugar.

Zhāng Méi ....   Jon Riley ....

> **Zài Zhōngwén lǐ ...**
>
> there's no direct translation of *please*. *Yes, please* is **Hǎo, xièxie**, and *please (do something)* is **qǐng** as in **qǐng zuò**. **Qǐng** literally means *invite* and can be used to offer to buy a drink: **Wǒ qǐng nǐ/nǐmen** *It's my round*. Sometimes, *please* is conveyed with **ba**: **Hē ba** *Please drink*.

3   1•60 Zhāng Méi visits Lín Guóqiáng the following day. Their conversation is below, but not in the right order. Rearrange the phrases, then listen to see if you got it right.

- **Nǐ hǎo, Zhāng Méi, qǐng jìn.**
- **Xièxie.**
- **Wǒ hěn hǎo. Qǐng zuò. Nǐ hē chá ma?**
- **Qǐng hē chá.**
- **Zhè ge chá hěn hǎohē.**
- **Xièxie, Lín xiānsheng, nín hǎo ma?**
- **Wǒ yào hóng chá.**

Making choices

1 1•61 Listen to the key language:

Nǐmen yào ...	Would you like ...
... chá háishi kāfēi?	... tea or coffee?
... bái (pútáojiǔ) háishi hóng (pútáojiǔ)?	... white (wine) or red (wine)?
Wǒmen dōu yào chá.	We'd <u>all</u>/<u>both</u> like tea.
Wǒ yě yīyàng.	The same for me.
Gān bēi!	Cheers!

2 1•62 Jon Riley goes back to see Lǐ Wěi the next day with German colleagues Elke Braun and Eric Hollmann. Listen to the conversation then make a note of what's offered to them and what they accept.

- .... **háishi** ....
- Jon .... Elke .... Eric ....

> **Zài Zhōngwén lǐ ...**
>
> in a question, *or* is **háishi**. When **háishi** appears in a question, **ma** is not needed at the end.
>
> **Nǐ yào chá háishi kāfēi?** *Would you like tea or coffee?*
>
> **Tāmen shì Yīngguórén háishi Měiguórén?** *Are they English or American?*
>
> G10

3 1•63 After work, Zhāng Méi is meeting Jon and a friend Lisa in a **kāfēiguǎn** *café*. Listen and tick what they have to drink.

	píjiǔ	kuàngquán shuǐ	bái pútáojiǔ	hóng pútáojiǔ	júzi zhī
Zhāng Méi					
Jon					
Lisa					

4 How would you offer someone these choices?

  a green tea or jasmine tea?
  b red or white wine?
  c mineral water or orange juice?
  d beer or cola?

put it all together

1   Choose an appropriate response from the box below.

   a   Xièxie
   b   Nín yào hē shénme?
   c   Qǐng zuò
   d   Nǐmen yào chá háishi kāfēi?
   e   Nǐ yào jiā niúnǎi ma?

   > Gān bēi   Hěn hǎo   Xièxie   Wǒ yào yī bēi lǜ chá
   > Bú kèqi   Bú yào, xièxie   Wǒmen dōu hē chá

2   What has been ordered to drink here?

   a   sān bēi hóng pútáojiǔ, yī píng kělè
   b   liǎng bēi hóng chá, wǔ bēi kāfēi, yī bēi bīng hóng chá
   c   jiǔ guàn júzi zhī, sì píng kuàngquán shuǐ
   d   yī píng píjiǔ, yī bēi bái pútáojiǔ, liǎng guàn kělè

3   For each of these, write the number in pinyin and replace the
   picture with the correct measure word.

   a   1   [image]   hóng pútáojiǔ   e   4   [image]   kāfēi

   b   6   [image]   píjiǔ   f   3   [image]   píjiǔ

   c   2   [image]   júzi zhī   g   5   [image]   bái pútáojiǔ

   d   7   [image]   nǎi chá   h   1   [image]   kuàngquán shuǐ

4   Rearrange the words to make sentences.

   a   shénme yào hē nín?
   b   zhè ge hǎohē hěn chá
   c   háishi yào nǐmen kuàngquán shuǐ júzi zhī?
   d   kělè yào píng yī wǒ

now you're talking!

1   **1•64** You're in a tea shop, about to order for yourself and two friends who don't speak Chinese.

- **Nǐmen hǎo. Nǐmen yào shénme?**
- ◆ Say you all want tea.
- **Nǐmen yào shénme chá? Hóng chá, lǜ chá háishi huā chá?**
- ◆ Order a green tea for yourself.
- **Tāmen yào shénme chá?**
- ◆ Say they want a black tea and a jasmine tea.
- **Hǎo de. ... Gěi nǐmen chá.**

2   **1•65** You've just arrived at Guómào Trading Company where you have an appointment.

- **Nín hǎo. Qǐng jìn, qǐng zuò.**
- ◆ Say thank you.
- **Bú xiè. Nín hē chá háishi kāfēi?**
- ◆ You'll have tea, please.
- **Nín yào lǜ chá háishi hóng chá?**
- ◆ Go for the black tea.
- **Nín yào jiā niúnǎi ma? Nín yào jiā táng ma?**
- ◆ You don't want them.
- **Gěi nín.**
- ◆ Say the tea's delicious.

3   **1•66** Now, in a **jiǔbā** with a friend, you're going to have the following conversation.

- Ask your friend if he'd like some beer. You're buying.
- ◆ He says he'd like red wine.
- Order a glass of red wine for him and a bottle of beer for yourself.
- ◆ When the drinks arrive, say *Cheers!*

quiz

1 When accepting the offer of a drink, how do you say *please* in Chinese?

2 How do you respond when someone says **xièxie** to you?

3 To say you'd like some red wine, would you add **bái** or **hóng** to **Wǒ yào ……. pútáojiǔ?**

4 If you hear **Qǐng zuò**, what are you being invited to do?

5 Would you use **bēi**, **ge**, **píng** or **guàn** when asking for two bottles of beer?

6 If you're not sure of the correct measure word, which should you go for?

7 To offer someone some tea or coffee, what would you need to add to **Nǐ yào chá ……………… kāfēi?**

8 If **Bú yào bīng, xièxie** is *No ice, thank you*, how would you say you don't want milk?

Now check whether you can …

- ask for a coffee or a cup of various types of tea
- order one or more cold drinks in a bar
- offer someone a drink
- accept or say no thank you when you're offered a drink
- pay a compliment on receiving a cup of tea
- respond when someone thanks you

The way to get used to measure words is to use them every day. When you have a coffee or a beer or a glass of water, say what you're drinking in Chinese and include the measure word after **yī** (or other numbers if you're with someone else).

As your vocabulary increases you'll come across more MWs which you can add to your list of things you regularly say in Chinese. For example, **běn** is used for any kind of book, **bāo** for anything in a packet and **liàng** for things with wheels, e.g. cars, buses, bikes.

Checkpoint 1

1

qǐng jìn

bú kèqi

nǐ hǎo

wǎn'ān

hěn gāoxìng rènshi nǐ

wǒ hěn hǎo, xièxie

zhè shì wǒde míngpiàn

míngtiān jiàn

nǐ duō dà le?

mǎmǎhūhū

wǒ bú yào, xièxie

zǎoshang hǎo

qǐng zuò

zhè shì wǒde wàigōng

zhè ge chá hěn hǎohē

Which expression would you use …

a to greet somebody in the morning
b when you're introduced to someone
c to say your tea's delicious
d to say you're very well
e to invite someone to sit down
f to decline something, for example a drink
g in reply to *thank you*
h to ask how old someone is
i to say goodnight
j when presenting a business card

2 Identify the odd one out.

a	pútáojiǔ	júzi zhī	jiǔbā	píjiǔ	kuàngquán shuǐ
b	èrshíqī	shísān	bǎi	liùshíyī	guó
c	Yīngwén	érzi	zhàngfu	nǚ'ér	mèimei
d	Yīnggélán	Sūgélán	Wēi'ěrshì	Àodàlìyà	Ài'ěrlán
e	bēi	ge	guàn	píng	shuǐ
f	zhǔxí	jīnglǐ	wàipó	tóngshì	zhǔrèn
g	dǎoyóu	péngyou	jìzhě	yīshēng	gōngchéngshī
h	niúnǎi	kāfēi	chá	táng	líng

3   The proprietor of your holiday hotel has asked if you'd help his teenage niece fill in a form for an English course in London. What are the questions you need to ask her before you can fill this in?

> **Name:** ....
> **Age:** ....
> **Nationality:** ....
> **Occupation:** ....

a   ....
b   ....
c   ....
d   ....

4   Are these answers right or wrong? Correct any wrong ones.

a   11 + 14 = **èrshí-liù**   b   40 + 7 = **sānshí-qī**
c   50 + 2 = **wǔshí-èr**   d   60 + 34 = **liùshí-bā**

A good way of practising low numbers is to throw two dice and say aloud the possible number combinations. For example:

3 **sān**
5 **wǔ**
35 **sānshíwǔ**
53 **wǔshísān**

Three dice will let you go further and practise the hundreds.

5   1•67 Listen to the international dialling codes for these countries and add the missing numbers. Can you guess what the countries are?

Xiānggǎng	00 852	**Rìběn**	00 ....
Yìndùníxīyà	00	**Tàiguó**	00 ....
Xīnjiāpō	00	**Yuènán**	00 ....
Mǎláixīyà	00	**Fēilǜbīn**	00 ....

Now say your phone number, complete with the international code.

6   **1•68** Practise saying the names of some of China's major cities, paying careful attention to the tones. Then listen to check your pronunciation.

Xī'ān	Luòyáng	Chóngqìng	Chéngdū
Hā'ěrbīn	Sūzhōu	Tiānjīn	Guǎngzhōu
Shēnzhèn	Xīshuāngbǎnnà		

7   **1•69** While waiting at Beijing Airport you overhear two young people getting to know each other. Listen, then complete this profile of Nicola by ticking the right information.

You'll hear a new question:

Nǐ lái Zhōngguó dùjià háishi gōngzuò? *Are you in China on holiday or for work?*

Nicola shì	☐ Yīngguórén	☐ Měiguórén
Nicola de māma shì	☐ Zhōngguórén	☐ Měiguórén
Nicola zài Zhōngguó	☐ dùjià	☐ gōngzuò
Tā	☐ èrshíyī suì	☐ èrshíqī suì
Tā shì	☐ xuésheng	☐ yīshēng
Tāde bàba shì	☐ yīshēng	☐ gōngchéngshī

Guóqiáng invites Nicola for a drink **Wǒ qǐng nǐ hē píjiǔ**. What does she have?

8 Here are the Chinese characters for the numbers 1 to 5:

一	二	三	四	五

Have a look at some more:

10	**shí**	十
11	**shíyī**	十一
20	**èrshí**	二十
25	**èrshíwǔ**	二十五

Can you say what the following are?

a 十三　　　　b 十五　　　　c 二十二　　　　d 三十

9 Now find some patterns relating to nationality.

Wǒ shì 我是　　　**Nǐ shì** 你是　　**Tā shì** 他是

Nǐ shì nǎ guó rén? 你是哪国人

Zhōngguó 中国	**Zhōngguórén** 中国人
Yīngguó 英国	**Yīngguórén** 英国人
Měiguó 美国	**Měiguórén** 美国人

Can you work out what these say?

a 我是中国人

b 他是美国人

10 Now for some drinks.

lǜ chá	绿茶	**kuàngquán shuǐ**	矿泉水
huā chá	花茶	**bái pútáojiǔ**	白葡萄酒
hóng chá	红茶	**hóng pútáojiǔ**	红葡萄酒

Decide which of these means red, white, tea and water.

a 茶　　　　b 水　　　　c 白　　　　d 红

Yǒu shìchǎng ma?

asking what there is in town

... and whereabouts it is

finding out how far places are

... and when they're open

Zài Zhōngguó ...

the local 旅游局 lǚyóu jú *tourist office* in the main towns are generally administrative bodies, so if you want to find out what to see and do, the hotel reception is your best starting point.

Distances are measured using the metric system, based on the **mǐ** *metre* and **gōnglǐ** *kilometre*. You might occasionally still hear **lǐ**, a traditional Chinese unit of distance now standardised to 500 metres. It features in the traditional name for the Great Wall of China **Wàn Lǐ Chángchéng**, literally *the 10,000 lǐ wall*, a symbolic name intended to convey the immeasurable nature of the Wall but which, in reality, underestimates the actual length.

Asking what there is in town

1   1•70 Listen to the key language:

Yǒu cānguǎn.	There's a restaurant.
Yǒu hěnduō cānguǎn.	There are many restaurants.
Qǐng wèn ...	Please may I ask ...
Yǒu shìchǎng ma?	Is there a market?
<u>**Zhèr**</u> **yǒu wǎngbā ma?**	Is there an internet café <u>here</u>?
Méi yǒu gōngyuán.	There isn't a park.

Zài Zhōngwén lǐ ...

yǒu means *have* and also *there is/there are*. The negative uses **méi**, rather than **bù** like other verbs in the present tense:

yǒu chāojí shìchǎng *there's a supermarket*; <u>**méi yǒu**</u> chāojí shìchǎng *there's no supermarket*.

wǒ **yǒu** yī ge érzi *I have one son*; wǒ <u>**méi yǒu**</u> háizi *I <u>don't have</u> children*.

In reply to a question using **yǒu** or **méi yǒu**, *yes* is **yǒu** and *no* is **méi yǒu**.

---

2   Have a look at this list of places and practise saying them.

shāngdiàn	**shìchǎng**	**chāojí shìchǎng**	**yínháng**	**wǎngbā**
商店	市场	超级市场	银行	网吧
shop	*market*	*supermarket*	*bank*	*internet café*

cānguǎn	**xīcānguǎn**	**gōngyuán**	**huāyuán**	**bówùguǎn**
餐馆	西餐馆	公园	花园	博物馆
restaurant	*Western restaurant*	*park*	*gardens*	*museum*

3   1•71 Tour guide Xin Liu tells a group of visitors some basic facts about her town. Listen and pick out the four places she mentions.

4   1•72 Now listen as people ask her questions, and tick or cross the availability of the following. **Fúzhuāng** means *clothes*.

internet café	Western restaurant
clothes market	museum

... and whereabouts it is

5 1•73 Listen to the key language:

Bówùguǎn	The museum
... zài <u>shì zhōngxīn</u>.	... is in the <u>town centre</u>.
... zài shì zhōngxīn <u>de běi biān</u>	... is <u>to the north</u> of the town centre
... zài yínháng duìmiàn.	... is opposite the bank.
... zài yínháng pángbiān.	... is next to the bank.

6 1•74 Xin Liu is using this map of the town centre to explain where places are. Check you know what the named places are, then listen and work out what A, B and C represent.

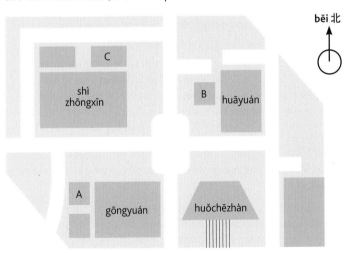

Zài Zhōngwén lǐ ...

zài is used to say where something is, translating words like *in*, *at* or *on* according to the context. It also translates *is/are in*, *at* or *on* without the need for the verb shì *to be*.

---

7 1•75 Listen as Xin Liu is asked again if there's a clothes market. In her reply you'll hear **huǒchēzhàn** *train station*. Is the market next to or opposite the station?

Finding out how far places are

1   1•76 Listen to the key language:

Fùjìn yǒu méi yǒu gōngyuán?   Is there a park <u>nearby</u>?
Gōngyuán lí zhèr <u>yuǎn</u> ma?   Is the park <u>far</u> from here?
Bù yuǎn, hěn jìn.   Not far, very near.
wǔ bǎi <u>mǐ</u>/liǎng <u>gōnglǐ</u> yuǎn   500 <u>metres</u>/2 <u>kilometres</u> away
zǒulù èrshí fēnzhōng   20 minutes' walk *Lit.* walk
   20 minutes

Zài Zhōngwén lǐ ...

Yǒu méi yǒu ...? is a very common alternative to **Yǒu ... ma?**
for *Is/Are there ...?* or *Have you got ...?*
Běijīng yǒu méi yǒu gōngyuán? *Are there parks in Beijing?*
Nǐ yǒu méi yǒu háizi? *Do you have children?*

The same structure (verb + negative + same verb) works with
other verbs too, e.g. **Shì bú shì ...?** as an alternative to **Shì ...**
ma? for *Are you/is he/she?* etc. This would be the equivalent of
Are you or are you not ...?

---

2   1•77 Xin Liu's group is exploring without her, and Harry's looking for
a bank. Listen and decide where it is and how long it will take him to
walk there.

3   1•78 Anna's looking for a supermarket. First, remind yourself which of
these words means supermarket:

● **shìchǎng**   ● **cānguǎn**   ● **chāojí shìchǎng**   ● **shāngdiàn**

Then listen and work out how far it is.

4   1•79 Anna then asks whether there's a **yóuyǒngchí** *swimming pool*
and is told it's <u>to the west</u> of the town centre: **Yóuyǒngchí zài shì**
zhōngxīn <u>de xī biān</u>. Listen and work out what she's told about
getting there.

... and when they're open

5 **1•80** Listen to the key language:

... jīntiān/míngtiān kāimén ma?		Is ... open today/tomorrow?
... xīngqīyī kāimén ma?		Is ... open on Monday?
... měi tiān kāimén.		.... is open every day.
... xīngqītiān guānmén.		....is closed on Sunday.

xīngqīyī	星期一	Monday
xīngqī'èr	星期二	Tuesday
xīngqīsān	星期三	Wednesday
xīngqīsì	星期四	Thursday
xīngqīwǔ	星期五	Friday
xīngqīliù	星期六	Saturday
xīngqītiān/xīngqīrì	星期天	Sunday

6 **1•81** Xin Liu is telling Harry which days the swimming pool and the **táocí bówùguǎn** *porcelain museum* are open and when there's a **zhǎnlǎnhuì** *exhibition* in town. Listen and fill the gaps. How would Harry relay this information in English?

- Yóuyǒngchí .... kāimén.
- Táocí bówùguǎn ...., ... hé .... guānmén.
- .... yǒu zhǎnlǎnhuì.

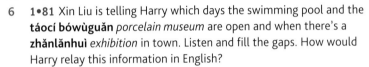

Zài Zhōngguó ...

the day is divided into five: **zǎoshang** early morning; **shàngwǔ** about 9am until noon; **zhōngwǔ** noon; **xiàwǔ** afternoon until about 6pm; **wǎnshang** after 6pm. These are used with **jīntiān**, **míngtiān** and the days of the week, e.g. **míngtiān xiàwǔ** *tomorrow afternoon*, **xīngqīwǔ wǎnshang** *Friday evening*.

7 **1•82** Listen to Xin Liu giving the opening hours for the **yóujú** *post office*, then number the following times 1 or 2 according to whether it's open or closed at that time.

1 yóujú ...... kāimén	2 yóujú ...... guānmén
xīngqīliù xiàwǔ	xīngqīliù wǎnshang
xīngqīliù shàngwǔ	xīngqītiān zǎoshang
xīngqītiān wǎnshang	

put it all together

1 Match the phrases.

a	**Gōngyuán bù yuǎn**	1	There's no supermarket nearby
b	**Méi yǒu wǎngbā**	2	There are lots of shops
c	**Bówùguǎn zài yínháng duìmiàn**	3	The museum is opposite the bank
d	**Fùjìn méi yǒu chāojí shìchǎng**	4	The bank is next to the market
e	**Zǒulù èrshìwǔ fēnzhōng**	5	The park isn't far
f	**Yǒu hěnduō shāngdiàn**	6	Twenty-five minutes' walk
g	**Yínháng zài shìchǎng pángbiān**	7	There's no internet café

2 Have a look at these notices then answer the questions.

Zhōngguó yínháng
Bank of China
xīngqīyī – xīngqīliù:
shàngwǔ 8:00 – xiàwǔ 5:00
xīngqītiān: shàngwǔ 9:00 – xiàwǔ 4:00

Xīnghǎi yīnyuè tīng
Xinghai Concert Hall
xīngqīwǔ – xīngqīliù:
wǎnshang 7:00–10:30

Táoyuán jùyuàn
Taoyuan Opera House
xīngqīyī – xīngqīwǔ: xiàwǔ 2:00–5:00
wǎnshang 6:30–10:00
xīngqīliù – xīngqītiān: xiàwǔ 2:00–5:00

Mínzú Huàláng
Gallery of Folk Art
xīngqīyī – xīngqīliù:
shàngwǔ 9:00 – xiàwǔ 6:00

a Which day is the Gallery of Folk Art closed?
b What are the opening hours for the Bank of China?
c What time can you see an opera on Friday?
d Is there a concert mid-week at the Xinghai Concert Hall?

3 Using **Wǒde chéngshì** (*town*) **yǒu/méi yǒu ...** *In my town there is/there isn't ...*, say whether your home town has some of the places mentioned in this unit. The measure word you'll need is **jiā**, e.g. **yǒu sān jiā yínháng** *there are 3 banks*.

now you're talking!

1   **1•83** You're in Shenzhen, and you ask a man waiting at a bus stop for some information.

- Say *Excuse me* and ask if there's a park.
- ◆ **Yǒu. Hěn jìn – wǔ bǎi mǐ.**
- Now ask if there are any shops here.
- ◆ **Yǒu hěnduō shāngdiàn; zài shì zhōngxīn.**
- Thank him and say goodbye.
- ◆ **Bú xiè. Zàijiàn.**

2   **1•84** Later, you need to contact home so you stop someone else.

- Say *Excuse me* and ask if there's an internet café nearby.
- ◆ **Méi yǒu. Wǎngbā zài shì zhōngxīn de běi biān. Yuǎn, hěn yuǎn, wǔ gōnglǐ.**
- Pity. Now ask if the post office is far from here.
- ◆ **Yóujú bù yuǎn. Zài shì zhōngxīn , yínháng pángbiān.**
- Repeat the information you've been given and thank him.
- ◆ **Bú kèqi.**
- Now ask if the bank's open today.
- ◆ **Jīntiān yínháng guānmén.**
- Ask if it's open tomorrow.
- ◆ **Shìde. Míngtiān kāimén.**

quiz

1 What do you add to the beginning of a question to make it more polite?

2 Which is the odd one out: **shìchǎng shāngdiàn yóuyǒngchí chāojí shìchǎng**? What does it mean?

3 In China, is 3pm classed as **zhōngwǔ** or **xiàwǔ**?

4 If something is described as **zài chāojí shìchǎng pángbiān**, is it next to or opposite the supermarket?

5 Can you think of another way of asking **Yǒu xīcānguǎn ma?**

6 What's the opposite of these words? **yǒu, kāimén, yuǎn**

7 Would you expect the Bank of China to be open **xīngqīliù shàngwǔ?**

8 What would you need to add to **Yǒu ... cānguǎn** to say there are *many* restaurants?

Now check whether you can ...

- approach someone politely
- understand and say the words for places in town
- ask if there's a particular place nearby
- understand basic phrases describing where a place is
- ask if a place is open
- recognise the days of the week
- recognise parts of the day

Practise the language of this unit by imagining you're telling a Chinese visitor when places are open where you live, for example, banks, supermarkets, swimming pool, library **túshūguǎn**. Writing the information down in pinyin, making sure you include the tone marks, will really help you to focus on the sounds – as well as to remember the words.

Shì zhōngxīn zài nǎr?

asking the way

... and following directions

talking about where people live

getting help to understand

Zài Zhōngguó ...

the points of the compass are **dōng** *east*, **nán** *south*, **xī** *west*, **běi** *north*, said in that order. They're regularly used when giving directions, and are a feature of numerous place names such as **Shāndōng**, **Xī'an** and, of course, **Běijīng** and **Nánjīng**, literally *north capital* and *south capital*, dating from when China was divided by the Yangtze river into two kingdoms. Historically, **zhōng** *central* was linked with **dōng**, **nán**, **xī** and **běi**, and **Zhōngguó** *China* literally means *Middle Kingdom*.

Other words that feature regularly in place names include **hǎi** *sea*, **hé** *river*, **hú** *lake*, **shān** *mountain*, **shěng** *province* and **shì** *city*.

Asking the way

1   2•1 Listen to the key language:

... zài nǎr?	Where is/are ...?
Zuìjìn de ... zài nǎr?	Where is/are the nearest ...?
... zài yī/èr/sān céng	...is/are on the ground/first/second floor
... zài lóushàng/lóuxià	... is/are upstairs/downstairs
... zài nǐde <u>zuǒ</u>/<u>yòu</u> biān	... is/are on your <u>left</u>/<u>right</u>
Jiù zài nàbiān.	It's/they're just over there.
Duìbuqǐ, wǒ bù dǒng/zhīdao.	Sorry, I don't understand/know.

2   2•2 In a shopping centre, Tom Stratton asks where the toilets are. Listen, tick what he's told, then explain in English where they are.

Cèsuǒ zài ... lóushàng ☐ lóuxià ☐ **èr céng** ☐ **sān céng** ☐ **sì céng** ☐

3   2•3 He doesn't find them so he asks again. You'll hear **Wǒ dong le**
I understand now. Listen and:

a   note in Chinese how the first person replies ....

b   say where the second person says they are ....

Zài Zhōngguó ...

floors are numbered as in the US, i.e. UK ground floor is **yī céng**, UK first floor is **èr céng** and so on; and they tend to be numbered *one*, *two*, *three*, etc. rather than *first*, *second*, *third*. To avoid the unlucky associations of 13 for westerners and 14 for local people, many high rise blocks no longer have a 13th or a 14th floor. Instead they have **12 céng**, **12 céng A** and **12 céng B**.

---

4   2•4 Having found the right floor, Tom gets the information he needs. Listen and fill the gaps. Are the toilets on the left or on the right?

● **Qǐng wèn, cèsuǒ ....?**

◆ **Cèsuǒ zài nǐde .... biān. Jiù .... nàbiān.**

 男 **nán**   女 **nǚ**

... and following directions

5 **2•5** Listen to the key language:

Qù ... zěnme zǒu?	How do I get to ...? *Lit.* ... how go?
Zǒu dào lùkǒu.	Go as far as the crossroads.
Zǒu dào <u>dì yī</u> ge hónglǜdēng.	Go as far as the <u>first</u> traffic lights.
Yìzhí zǒu.	Go straight on.
Wǎng <u>dōng/nán/xī/běi</u> zǒu.	Go<u>east</u>/<u>south</u>/<u>west</u>/<u>north</u>. *Lit.* Toward ... go.
Wǎng <u>zuǒ/yòu</u> guǎi.	Turn <u>left</u>/<u>right</u> *Lit.* Toward ... turn.
Duì/Bù duì.	That's correct/not correct.

6 **2•6** Tom's looking for the **huǒchēzhàn** *train station*. Listen and pick out from the above list the three pieces of information he's given.

7 **2•7** He now wants to go to Xuéyuàn Road and asks: **Qù Xuéyuàn Lù zěnme zǒu?** Listen to the reply and tick the correct option.

Wǎng	dōng	nán	xī	běi zǒu
Zǒu dào	lùkǒu	hónglǜdēng		
Wǎng	dōng	xī	zuǒ	yòu guǎi
Xuéyuàn Lù zài	zuǒ	yòu biān		

Zài Zhōngwén lǐ ...

to say *first, second, third* etc, you simply put **dì** before the number: **dì yī** *first*, **dì èr** *second*, **dì wǔ** *fifth*. The normal measure word is needed before a noun: **dì èr ge hónglǜdēng** *the second traffic lights*.

---

8 **2•8** The directions were wrong. Explaining he's lost: **Wǒ mí lù le**, Tom asks again. Listen and work out whether Xuéyuàn Road is A, B or C on the map.

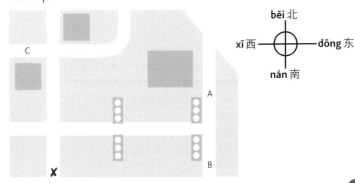

Talking about where people live

1   2•9 Listen to the key language:

Nǐ zhù zài nǎr?	Where do you live? *Lit.* you live in where?
Wǒ/Wǒmen zhù zài Shànghǎi.	I/We live in Shanghai.
Wǒ dìdi bú zhù zài Shànghǎi.	My brother doesn't live in Shanghai.
Nǐ dìdi zhù zài nǎr?	Where does your brother live?
Tā zhù zài jiāoqū/hǎi biān.	He/She lives in the suburbs/by the sea.
Tāmen zhù zài nóngcūn.	They live in the country.

2   2•10 Féng Yīmín, a Chinese student in the UK, is asking a group of language students where they live. Listen and tick who lives where. Listen out for **yě** *also*.

	town centre	country	suburbs	seaside
George				
Jacquie				
Fran				
Thomas				
Lizzie				

3   2•11 Yīmín then says where she and some other people live. Check that you remember who the following are, then listen and make a note of where they all live. You'll hear **dànshì** *but*.

Féng Yīmín ....   **Tā jiějie** ....

Tā bàba hé māma ....   **Tā yéye hé nǎinai** ....

Zài Zhōngwén lǐ ...

unlike in many other languages, verbs, e.g. **zhù** *to live*, **gōngzuò** *to work*, **zhīdao** *to know*, **dǒng** *to understand*, **shì** *to be*, stay unchanged regardless of who's talking or being talked about.

To make a sentence negative in the present tense, you put **bù** before the verb: **Wǒ (bù) zhù zài Shànghǎi** *I (don't) live in Shanghai*. The only exception is **yǒu** *to have*, which becomes **méi yǒu**.   **G9**

Getting help to understand

4 2•12 Listen to the key language:

Qǐng zài shuō yībiàn.	Please say it again.
Qǐng shuō màn yìdiǎn.	Please speak more slowly.
Nǐ huì shuō Yīngyǔ ma?	Can you speak English?
Bú huì/Huì. Huì shuō yìdiǎn.	No/Yes. I can speak a little.
Nǐde Yīngyǔ hěn hǎo.	Your English is very good.
Nǎli, nǎli!	Not at all!

5 2•13 Listen as Yīmìn introduces her friend Měilì, who talks about her **gōngyù** *apartment*.

a Where is it? .... b Which floor is it on? ....

6 2•14 Měilì continues but George loses the drift. Read their conversation, anticipating how the new words in the box will sound, listen with the text, then listen again with your book closed.

- **Wǒ shēng zài Sūzhōu, xiànzài zhù zài Shànghǎi.**
- **Qǐng zài shuō yībiàn.**
- **Wǒ zhù zài Shànghǎi, dànshì wǒ shēng zài Sūzhōu.**
- **Duìbuqǐ Měilì, wǒ bù dǒng. Nǐ huì shuō Yīngyǔ ma?**
- **Huì shuō Yìdiǎn.** I was born in Sūzhōu but now – **xiànzài** – I live in Shànghǎi.
- **Nǐde yīngyǔ hěn hǎo!**
- **Nǎli, nǎli.**

> **Wǒ shēng** *I was born*; **xiànzài** *now*

Zài Zhōnggwén lǐ ...

adding **wén** or **yǔ** *language* to the first syllable of many countries gives you the language: **Zhōngguó** *China*, **Zhōngwén** *Chinese*; **Yīngguó** *UK*, **Yingwén/Yīngyǔ** *English*; **Fǎguó** *France*, **Fǎwén/Fǎyǔ** *French*, **Rìběn** *Japan*, **Rìwén/Rìyǔ** *Japanese*.

For some languages, **wén/yǔ** is added to the entire country name: **Xībānyá** *Spain*, **Xībānyáwén/Xībānyáyǔ** *Spanish*. **Yǔ** refers more to spoken language and **wén** to written language.

put it all together

1 Find the corresponding Chinese phrase. Which one is left over? What does it mean?

a	Please say it again	1	**Qǐng shuō màn yìdiǎn**
b	Do you live in Germany?	2	**Nǐ shuō Déwén ma?**
c	I don't know	3	**Wǒ bù dǒng**
d	I speak a little bit of Chinese	4	**Wǎng dōng guǎi**
e	Please speak more slowly	5	**Wǒ bù zhīdao**
f	Do you speak German?	6	**Nǐ zhù zài Déguó ma?**
g	I don't understand	7	**Wǒ shuō yìdiǎn Zhōngwén**
		8	**Qǐng zài shuō yībiàn**

2 Fill the gaps with the words in the box.

a **Nǐ .... Yīngyǔ ma?**
b **Cèsuǒ .... lóuxià.**
c **Nǐmen .... zài nǎr?**
d **................. dào lùkǒu.**
e **Duìbuqǐ, wǒ bù ....**
f **Nǐ .... shuō Yīngyǔ ma?**

zhù	zhīdao
shuō	zǒu
huì	zài

3 Rearrange the following into a conversation.

a **Qǐng zài shuō yībiàn.**
b **Bú kèqì.**
c **Duìbuqǐ, fùjìn yǒu méi yǒu yínháng?**
d **Xièxie.**
e **Zǒu dào hónglǜdēng, wǎng yòu guǎi.**
f **Zǒu dào hónglǜdēng, wǎng yòu guǎi.**
g **Qù shì zhōngxīn zěnme zǒu?**
h **Yínháng zài shì zhōngxīn.**

now you're talking!

1   2•15 You're in a department store and can't see any signs.

- Ask a shopper where the nearest toilet is.
- ◆ **Cèsuǒ zài lóushàng, wǔ céng.**
- Ask her to repeat that.
- ◆ **Cèsuǒ zài lóushàng, wǔ céng.**
- Thank her – and tell your companion in English what she
  said.

2   2•16 You get lost on the way back to your hotel.

- Stop a passer-by and ask if he speaks English.
- ◆ **Duìbuqǐ. Bú huì.**
- Ask him how to get to the Zhōngshān Hotel.
- ◆ **Wǎng dōng zǒu, dào dì èr ge hónglǜdēng, wǎng yòu
  guǎi.**
- Say sorry, you don't understand.
- ◆ **Wǎng dōng zǒu, dào dì èr ge hónglǜdēng, wǎng yòu
  guǎi, yìzhí zǒu, jiù shì Zhōngshān Fàndiàn.**
- Ask if it's far.
- ◆ **Bù yuǎn, zǒulù shíwǔ fēnzhōng.**

3   2•17 Later, you get talking to a student staying at the
     Zhōngshān Hotel.

- Ask him where he lives.
- ◆ **Wǒ zhù zài Xiānggǎng.**
- Ask if his mother and father also live in Hong Kong.
- ◆ **Bù, tāmen zhù zài Shànghǎi. Wǒmen quán jiā dōu zhù
  zài nàr.**
- Say sorry, you don't understand **quán jiā**.
- ◆ **Quán jiā – bàba hé māma, jiějie, yéye hé nǎinai ...
  wàigōng, wàipó ...**
- Now you get it, **quán jiā** means *whole family*. Say you
  understand.
- ◆ **Nǐ Zhōngwén shuō de hěn hǎo!**
- Accept the compliment modestly – as is the custom
  in China.

quiz

1 What's the literal meaning of **Dōngjīng**, the Chinese name for Tokyo?

2 Would you expect to see 女 on the women's or the men's toilet?

3 **Xiànchāo jī** means *cashpoint*. What's the difference between **Xiànchāo jī zài nǎr?** and **Zuìjìn de xiànchāo jī zài nǎr?**

4 Should you turn left or right if someone tells you **wǎng zuǒ guǎi**?

5 How might you respond to a compliment?

6 Which is the only verb that doesn't use **bù** for the negative in the present tense?

7 In the UK, what's the equivalent of **shíyī céng**?

8 Given that **gōngzuò** means *to work*, how would you say *I work in Beijing*, and ask *Do you work in Hong Kong*?

Now check whether you can …

- ask where a place is and how to get there
- follow some basic directions
- ask someone where they live
- say where you and others live
- ask someone to repeat what they've said and to speak more slowly
- check if someone speaks English
- say you speak a little Chinese
- say you don't know or don't understand

Practise what you've just learnt and extend it by using **zài nǎr?** and **zěnme zǒu?** to ask where all the places you learnt in Unit 5 are and how you'd get to them. Then have a go at saying where you and various friends and members of your family live, and whether you speak the languages mentioned on page 55. You could also try writing a paragraph about one particular person, starting with **tā**.

Duōshao qián?

understanding prices in renminbi

asking for what you want

shopping in a department store

bargaining

Zài Zhōngguó ...

shops are open every day, including Chinese New Year, from around 8.30 in the morning until late evening. And you'll find shopping opportunities everywhere, whether from street vendors, **shāngdiàn** and **shìchǎng** selling anything from fresh produce to herbal medicines to silk and cashmere, or exclusive **gòuwù zhōngxīn** *shopping malls* selling international designer labels and exquisite works of art.

In markets and small shops, bargaining over prices is not only acceptable but expected, and payment is in cash. Indeed, away from the big centres, it's a good idea never to assume you can pay by credit card.

Understanding prices in renminbi

Zài Zhōngguó ...

the official currency is **renminbi** (RMB), meaning The People's Currency. There are 3 units: 1 **yuán** = 10 **jiǎo** = 100 **fēn**, although prices in tourist spots tend to be in round **yuán**.

The **yuán** is written ¥, and prices are written with a full stop between **yuán** and the other units: ¥25.75. Informally, **yuán** and **jiǎo** are called **kuài** and **máo**.

1   **2•19** Listen to these prices in renminbi:

¥1.00	**yī yuán**	¥10.30	**shí yuán sān jiǎo**
¥0.10	**yī jiǎo**	¥10.34	**shí yuán sān jiǎo sì fēn**
¥0.01	**yī fēn**	¥50.00	**wǔshí yuán**
¥10.00	**shí yuán**	¥85.75	**bāshíwǔ yuán qī jiǎo wǔ fēn**

2   Now, have a go at saying these prices.

a ¥8.00	b ¥0.87	c ¥19.50
d ¥42.00	e ¥64.55	f ¥90.99

3   **2•20** Listen to the key language:

Nín mǎi shénme?   What would you like? *Lit.* you buy what?
.... duōshao qián?   How much is/are the ...? *Lit.* how much

4   **2•21** First, get familiar with the names of these fruits. Then listen to people shopping in a **shuǐguǒ diàn** *greengrocer's* and jot down the cost of the various fruits. You'll hear **yī jīn** *per jīn* (a **jīn** = 500 grammes).

píngguǒ   **xiāngjiāo**   **lìzhī**   **mángguǒ**   **bōluó**

¥ ....   ¥ ....   ¥ ....   ¥ ....   ¥ ....

Asking for what you want

1   **2•22** Listen to the key language:

Yào duōshao?	How much/many do you want?
Wǒ yào (mǎi) …	I want (to buy) …
Wǒ mǎi …	I'll have *Lit.* I buy …
… zhè ge/nà ge	… this one/that one
… liǎng ge zhè ge/bā ge nà ge	… 2 of these/8 of those
Hái yào biéde ma?	Would you like anything else?

2   Here's Hannah Cheng's shopping list. Find out what the items are, using the glossary, and work out how they're pronounced.

> **fángshàiyóu**
> **màozi**
> **míngxìnpiàn**
> **qiǎokèlì**
> **lǚyóu dìtú**

3   **2•23** Listen to Hannah in the **xiǎomàibù** *corner shop* and note which item she asks for first and what the cost is.

> ### Zài Zhōngwén lǐ …
>
> **yào** literally means *want* or *need*, but also conveys the English *would like* in a shopping situation. It can be used with an item or with another verb: **wǒ yào màozi** / *want/need a hat*; **wǒ yào mǎi màozi** *I'd like to buy a hat*. In reply to a question asking if you want/would like something, *Yes* is **Yào** and *No* is **Bú yào**.

4   **2•24** Before listening to Hannah asking for the rest of the items, try to anticipate what she might say. When you've listened to the conversation a few times, link each of these phrases with an item from her list, then check with the transcript. Also note how much she spent **yígòng** *altogether*, including the postcards.

- **Wǒ yào …**
- **Wǒ mǎi zhè ge …**
- **Yígòng ¥……………**

- **Yǒu … ma?**
- **… duōshao qián?**

Shopping in a department store

1   **2•25** Listen to the key language:

Wǒ zài zhǎo ...	I'm looking for ...
Wǒ xiǎng kànkan nà ge.	I'd like to have a look at that one.
Wǒ <u>kěyǐ</u> shìshi ma?	<u>May</u> I try it on?
Tài <u>dà/xiǎo</u> le.	It's too <u>big/small</u>.
Yǒu dà/xiǎo hào ma?	Have you got a big/small size?
Yǒu qítā yánsè ma?	Have you got other colours?

Zài Zhōngwén lǐ ...

xiǎng is an alternative to **yào** to convey *would like* when followed by another verb.

Duplicating a verb introduces a casual sense or shorter duration of action: **kàn** *to look*, **kànkan** *to have a look*, **shì** *to try (on)*, **shìshi** *to have a try*, **xiǎng** *think*, **xiǎngxiang** *to think it over*. The repeated verb is unstressed.

---

2   **2•26** Li Guang is at a **bǎihuò shāngdiàn** *department store*, looking for a **lǐngdài** *tie* made of **zhēnsī** *silk* and also a **pījiān** *pashmina* for his girlfriend. The colours available include:

bái(sè) ☐   **hēi(sè)** ■   **hóng(sè)** ■

lán(sè) ■   **lǜ(sè)** ■   **huáng(sè)** ■

Listen to both conversations and make a note in English of the colours he buys.

lǐngdài ....
pījiān ....

> **Shìyījiān zài nǎr?**
> *Where's the changing room?*

3   **2•27** Li Guang then goes to buy a **chènshān** *shirt*. The sizes on offer are:
xiǎo hào *S*, **zhōng hào** *M*, **dà hào** *L*, **jiā dà hào** *XL*

Listen and tick whether these statements are true or false.

		True	False
a	He wants a blue shirt	▫	▫
b	He tries size medium first	▫	▫
c	It's too small for him	▫	▫

Bargaining

1   **2•28** Listen to the key language:

Hěn piàoliang.	(It's/they're) very beautiful.
Tài guì le.	(It's/they're) too <u>expensive</u>.
Piányi yìdiǎn ba?	Can you bring the price down a bit?
Zuìdī jià duōshao?	What's your lowest price? *Lit.* lowest price how much?
... yuán, zěnmeyàng?	How about ... yuan?
Hǎo ba.	Agreed, OK.

2   **2•29** In a **gōngyì měishù diàn** *arts and crafts shop*, Jack falls for a landscape painting and asks his friend Xiaoyue what it's called in Chinese:

- **Zhè ge Zhōngwén jiào shénme?**
- **Shānshuǐ huà.**

They talk to the assistant and Xiaoyue negotiates the price. Listen to their conversation, tick off any of the above key phrases that you hear, and note the price they finally agree on. You'll hear the word **qiān** *thousand*.

¥...................

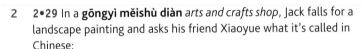

Zài Zhōngwén lǐ ...

adjectives of one syllable are used as in English: **xiǎo zhēnzhū** *a small pearl*, **dà fēngzheng** *a big kite*; but when the description involves more than one syllable, **de** is added after the adjectives: **piàoliang de zhēnzhū** *a beautiful pearl*; **hěn dà de fēngzheng** *a very big kite*. **Shì** *to be* is not used with adjectives.   **G5**

3   **2•30** Later, by himself in the market, Jack buys some **zhēnzhū ěrhuán** *pearl earrings* for his girlfriend. Listen and make a note of

a   the original asking price ¥......
b   how much he ends up paying ¥......

put it all together

1   If you buy three items, costing the following amounts, and pay for them all with a ¥100 note, how much change should you expect? How do you say it in Chinese?

èrshí yuán liù jiǎo, jiǔ yuán wǔ jiǎo, sìshíbā yuán yī jiǎo sān fēn

2   Which is the odd one out and why?

   a **guì, lán, hóng, hēi, bái**
   b **xiāngjiāo, qiǎokèlì, bōluó, píngguǒ, lìzhī**
   c **shuǐguǒ diàn, shāngdiàn, zhēnsī, shìchǎng, gòuwù zhōngxīn**
   d **piàoliang, zhōng, jiā dà, xiǎo, dà**
   e **chènshān, lǐngdài, pījiān, màozi, míngxìnpiàn**

3   Fill the gaps with the words in the box.

   | wǒmen lǜ ma |
   | mǎi zhè shìshi |
   | zhǎo yǒu |

   a **Nín xiǎng .... shénme?**
   b **Wǒ zài .... chènshān.**
   c **................ shì zhēnsī chènshān.**
   d **............. qítā yánsè ....?**
   e **............. yǒu báisè, lánsè, huángsè, ... sè.**
   f **Wǒ mǎi lánsè de chènshān. Wǒ kěyǐ .... ma?**

4   Rearrange the following to create a dialogue in a market.

   a **Duōshao qián?**
   b **Tài guì le! Piányí yìdiǎn ba?**
   c **Zhè ge hěn piàoliang.**
   d **Wǒ yào mǎi fēngzheng.**
   e **Nín mǎi shénme?**
   f **Hǎo ba.**
   g **Èr bǎi yuán, zěnmeyàng?**
   h **Èr bǎi wǔshí yuán.**

   What's being bought? How much is it bought for?

now you're talking!

1 2•31 Imagine you're visiting Suzhou and doing a bit of shopping. First you want something to eat.

- **Nǐ hǎo. Nǐ mǎi shénme?**
- You fancy some bananas. Ask how much they are.
- **Sān kuài yī jīn.**
- Buy 500 grammes of bananas.
- **Hái yào biéde ma?**
- Point to the pomegranates and say you'll have two of those. Then, in the shop next door, you spot some chocolate. Ask how much it is.
- **Bā yuán wǔ jiǎo.**
- You missed that. Ask if she'll repeat it.

2 2•32 Now for some presents from the department store.

- **Nín mǎi shénme?**
- Explain you're looking for a silk tie. Indicate one and add that you'd like to look at this one.
- **Hěn piàoliang de lǐngdài.**
- Ask if they have it in other colours.
- **Wǒmen yǒu lánsè, hóngsè, lǜsè, huángsè hé.**

3 2•33 Now to the jewellery market where you're going to do a spot of bargaining over a pearl necklace **zhēnzhū xiàngliàn.**

- **Hěn piàoliang de xiàngliàn – dà zhēnzhū. Liǎng qiān liù bǎi yuán.**
- Tell your friend in English how much it costs. Now tell the seller that it's too expensive.
- **Bú guì!**
- Ask if they'll bring the price down a bit. Suggest 1,200 yuan.
- **Hǎo ba.**
- Say thank you, then say goodbye.

quiz

1 How many **jiǎo** are there in a **yuán**? And how many **jīn** in a kilo?

2 What information does **Hái yào biéde ma** ask for?

3 Which of these verbs would you NOT use to say what you want in a shop? **xiǎng, zhù, yào, mǎi, shuō**

4 How would you ask for *five of those*?

5 What size do you think **liǎng ge jiā dà mǎ** is?

6 How do you answer *No* to the following? **Nǐ shì xuésheng ma? Nǐ yào qiǎokèlì ma? Nǐ yǒu háizi ma?**

7 Given that a jacket is **shàngyī** and pure wool is **chúnmáo**, how would you say you're looking for a wool jacket?

8 And if **hòu** means thick, how do you explain that it's too thick?

Now check whether you can ...

- ask how much something costs
- understand the answer in RMB
- ask for an item by name in a shop
- ask for this one/that one; one or more of these/those
- ask if you can have a look at something
- ask if you can try something on
- explain that something is (too) big, small or expensive
- ask for a bigger/smaller size or different colours
- bargain on a price

Word association can double the amount of vocabulary you retain. For example, you could link in your mind words in similar categories, such as **chènshān** and **lǐngdài**, or **míngxìnpiàn** and **yóupiào** *stamps*. When you learn an adjective, learn any obvious opposite as well: **xiǎo** and **dà**, **bái** and **hēi**.

And if you go to China or know any Chinese speakers, make sure you take every opportunity to add to your bank of words by asking ask **Zhè ge Zhōngwén jiào shénme?**

Checkpoint 2

1 **2•34-36** Listen to three people being given directions in their hotel reception. Follow their route on the map and write down in Pinyin and English the place they're going to and the letter which corresponds to it on the map.

a .... b .... c ....

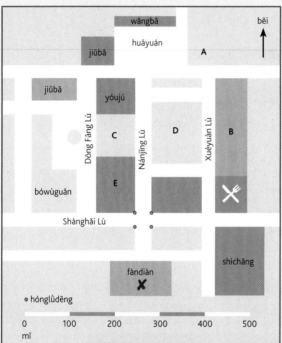

2 Look at the map again, decide if these statements are true or false and correct any false ones. **Jiā** is the measure word for shops, offices, restaurants, etc.

	true	false
a **Yǒu sān jiā jiǔbā.**	☐	☐
b **Méi yǒu gōngyuán.**	☐	☐
c **Bówùguǎn zài shuǐguǒdiàn duìmiàn.**	☐	☐

3 2•37 The following are foreign words adapted into Chinese. Guess
what they mean and check your answers in the glossary.

Then listen and check whether the prices you hear are the same as the
ones on the list. Tick the correct ones and change the wrong ones.

1 kǎbùqínuò ¥15 ☐
2 hànbǎo bāo ¥31 ☐
1 bǐsà bǐng ¥24.50 ☐
1 xiāngbīn ¥97 ☐
1 báilándì ¥85 ☐
3 wēishìjì ¥69 ☐

4 Starting with Monday, put these days in order.

> **xīngqītiān**   **xīngqīsì**   **xīngqī'èr**   **xīngqīliù**
> **xīngqīyī**   **xīngqīwǔ**   **xīngqīsān**

5 Can you work out what these numbers are? You might like to refer
back to pages 26 and 42.

a 十四   **b** 九十   **c** 五十五   **d** 七十三   **e** 六十二

Now see if you can write these in Chinese characters.

f 10   **g** 22   **h** 80   **i** 16

6 Match each sentence to the place in which you're most likely to hear it.

> **shuǐguǒ diàn**   **bówùguǎn**   **fàndiàn**
> **jiǔbā**   **bǎihuò shāngdiàn**

a **Zhǎnlǎnhuì měi tiān kāimén.**
b **Cāngguǎn zài sì céng.**
c **Wǒ kéyǐ shìshi zhè jiàn chènshān ma?**
d **Nǐ hē hóng pútáojiǔ háishì bái pútáojiǔ?**
e **Wǒ mǎi yī ge mángguǒ hé yī gōngjīn xiāngjiāo.**

7 Which of these might you use …

> Qǐng zài shuō yībiàn

> Duìbuqǐ

> Qǐng shuō màn yìdiǎn

> Wǒ xiǎng kànkan zhè ge

> Kěyǐ shìshi ma?

> Tài guì le, piányi yìdiǎn ba

> Yǒu dà hào ma?

> Nǐ huì shuō Yīngyǔ ma?

a if you want to try something on?
b to find out if someone speaks English?
c if you're looking for a large size?
d when you're bargaining over a price?
e when you'd like to have a look at something in a shop?
f to get someone to speak more slowly?
g to have something repeated?
h to say you're sorry.

8 Put the words below into seven groups, according to meaning. There
will be three words in each group.

dōng   dà   chènshān   shìchǎng   xīcānguǎn
hǎi biān   jiǔbǎ   nóngcūn   màozi   xiāngjiāo
chāojí shìchǎng   lǐngdài   nán   cānguǎn   jiāoqū
shāngdiàn   guì   běi   píngguǒ   xiǎo   lìzhī

9 Take a close look at the characters for the following **shuǐguǒ** *fruit*.

 苹果 **píngguǒ**   橘子 **júzi**

 芒果 **mángguǒ**   橙子 **chéngzi**

 杨桃 **yángtáo**   桃子 **táozi**

 蜜瓜 **mì guā**   梨子 **lízi**

Now match these characters to their pinyin.

a 椰子   b 樱桃   c 西瓜   d 柠檬

xī guā   **níngméng**   **yēzi**   **yīngtáo**

10 After looking at these characters for various **diàn** *shops*, work out
what the ones in the list below them mean in English.

greengrocer's	**shuǐguǒ diàn**	水果店
bakery	**miànbāo diàn**	面包店
grocery shop	**záhuò diàn**	杂货店
flower shop	**huā diàn**	花店
shoe shop	**xié diàn**	鞋店
toy shop	**wánjù diàn**	玩具店
furniture store	**jiājù diàn**	家俱店
bookshop	**shū diàn**	书店
stationery store	**wén jù diàn**	文具店

a 店   b 书   c 花

d 面包   e 鞋   f 文具

Yǒu kòng fángjiān ma?

finding a hotel room

... and saying how long you want to stay

checking in

making requests

Zài Zhōngguó ...

there are several words for hotels: **fàndiàn**, **jiǔdiàn**, **bīnguǎn**, and the accommodation available to visitors ranges from **wǔ xīng jí háohuá bīnguǎn** *5-star luxury hotels* to **qīngnián lǚshè** *youth hostels* and **zhāodàisuǒ** *economy guesthouses* – with prices and facilities varying accordingly. The best places for advice and information are the internet and the local **lǚxíngshè** *travel service*.

Large international hotels generally provide both Chinese- and Western-style breakfast, included in the room price. In smaller hotels, you need to check if breakfast is provided and/or included.

Finding a hotel room

1 2•38 Listen to the key language:

Yǒu (kòng) fángjiān ma?	Is there a room (available)?
Wǒ yào ...	I want ...
... dānrén/shuāngrén/ liǎngrén fángjiān	... a single/double/twin room
... dài kōngtiáo	... with air conditioning
... dài yùshì	... with en suite bathroom
Bāo zǎocān ma?	Is breakfast included?

Zài Zhōngwén lǐ ...

fángjiān *room* is often shortened to jiān when coupled with dānrén or shuāngrén, e.g. dānrén jiān or even dānjiān. Jiān is also the measure word for a room: yī jiān fángjiān, zhè jiān fángjiān.

2 2•39 Listen to four people enquiring about rooms at the 3-star Mín Háng Fàndiàn then, on the grid, tick what kind of accommodation they want.

Huānyíng guānglín
Welcome

Zhāng Yàn					
Lǐ Míng					
Zhōu Ān					
Chén Hè					

3 2•40 Listen as Chén Hè goes on to ask about breakfast, and jot down

a in Pinyin the reply to **Bāo zǎocān ma?** What do you think no would be?

b in English what floor the restaurant is on.

... and saying how long you want to stay

4   2•41 Listen to the key language:

Nín **shénme shíhou** zhù?	<u>When</u> do you want to stay?
Nín zhù jǐ wǎn?	How many nights do you want to stay?
zhǐ yào jīnwǎn	just for tonight
cóng jīntiān **dào** xīngqī'èr	<u>from</u> today <u>until</u> Tuesday
Wǒ (yào) zhù ...	I (want to) stay ...
... sān ge wǎnshang/yī ge xīngqī.	... for 3 nights/1 week.
... dào sānyuè liù hào.	... until the 6th of March.
Duìbuqǐ, wǒmen zhù mǎn le.	Sorry, we're full.

5   2•42 Check you understand the following, then listen as people say how long they want their rooms for, numbering the three you hear in the order you hear them.

wǔ ge wǎnshang..... yī ge xīngqī..... cóng jīntiān dào xīngqīsān .....
zhǐ yào jīnwǎn.......... liǎng ge wǎnshang ......

Zài Zhōngwén lǐ ...

for the months, you simply put the numbers 1–12 in front of yuè *moon, month*:

yīyuè *January*	èryuè *February*	sānyuè *March*
sìyuè *April*	wǔyuè *May*	liùyuè *June*
qīyuè *July*	bāyuè *August*	jiǔyuè *September*
shíyuè *October*	shíyīyuè *November*	shíèryuè *December*

The order for dates is: **nián** *year*, **yuè** *month*, **hào** *date*, **tiān** *day of the week*: èrlínglíngbā nián èryuè shíbā hào xīngqītiān
Sunday 18 February, 2008

---

6   2•43 The receptionist at the Mín Háng is taking bookings over the phone – you'll hear her say **Wèi** *Hello*, and **Qǐng shāo děng** *One moment, please*. Listen and note when the callers want rooms and which one can't be accommodated.

> Wèi, nǐ hǎo, shì Mín Háng Fàndiàn

a .... b .... c ....

Checking in

1 2•44 Listen to the key language:

Wǒ yùdìng le fángjiān.	I have a reservation.
Nín guì xìng?	Your surname?
Qǐng gěi wǒ nínde hùzhào.	Please give me your passport.
Qǐng tián zhè zhāng biǎo.	Please fill this form.
Qǐng gēn wǒ lái.	Please come with me.
Gěi nín yàoshi.	Here's your key. *Lit.* Give you key.

2 2•45 Listen to a visitor checking in at the Dōngfāng Hotel and tick the correct option.

a His surname is   Qián   Qíng   Qín   Xíng

b He's booked a   single   double   twin

c He's staying for   1 night   2 nights   4 nights   1 week

d He's asked to   fill in a form   show his passport

e His **fángjiān hàomǎ** *room number* is 617   716   670   706

3 2•46 Listen to three more people checking in, and note the details of their room on the grid.

			wǎnshang	**fángjiān hàomǎ**
Lǐ xiānsheng				
Zhāng xiǎojie				
Gāo tàitai				
Chén Hè				

4 Listen again and note where the **diàntī** *lifts* are. ....

Making requests

1   **2•47** Listen to the key language:

Wǒ néng/kěyǐ … ma?	Can/May I …
yòng xìnyòngkǎ fù	pay by credit card?
bǎ wǒde xínglǐ liú zài zhèr	leave my luggage here?
Nǐ néng bù néng …	Can you …
… liù diǎn jiào xǐng wǒ?	… wake me at 6am?
… gěi wǒ jiào yī liàng chūzūchē?	… call a taxi <u>for</u> me?
Dāngrán kěyǐ.	Of course.

2   **2•48** Wáng Chūn is getting ready to leave the Dōngfāng Hotel. Listen to his conversation with the receptionist Xiāo Xiá, and note in English the two things he asks her.

a ………………………………….…   b ……………………………………………

Zài Zhōngwén lǐ …

as in English, **néng** *can* and **kěyǐ** *may* are used in a similar way:
Wǒ néng yòng xìnyòngkǎ fù ma? *Can I pay by card?* **Wǒ kěyǐ shìshi ma?** *May I try it on?*

To ask somebody else to do something, e.g. wake you at
5 o'clock, you can use **Nǐ néng … ma?**, **Nǐ néng bù néng …?** or
Qǐng …: Nǐ néng wǔ diǎn jiào xǐng wǒ ma?; **Nǐ néng bù néng wǔ
diǎn jiào xǐng wǒ?**; **Qǐng wǔ diǎn jiào xǐng wǒ.**

---

3   **2•49** Xiāo Xiá is kept busy all day with requests from guests. Listen to her at work and number any of the following that you hear.

yòng xìnyòngkǎ fù	
yòng bǎoxiǎnxiāng *use the safe*	
yòng jiànshēnfáng *use the gym*	
yòng hùliánwǎng jiēkǒu *use the internet*	
yòng zhè ge diànhuà *use this phone*	
gěi wǒ jiào yī liàng chūzūchē	
bǎ wǒde xínglǐ liú zài zhèr	

put it all together

Wǒmen zhù	**Qǐng**	**Nǐ néng bù néng**	**Gěi nǐ**
Wǒmen néng ... ma		**Wǒ yào**	**Wǒ kěyǐ ... ma**

1 Which phrase from the box would you use to:

a say you want or need something,
b ask someone if they can do something for you,
c say you (and somebody else) are staying for ...
d ask if you may do something,
e hand something over,
f request someone to do something,
g ask if you (and somebody else) can ...

2 Complete the following.

a **Yǒu kòng .... ma?**

b **Wǒ yào ....**

c **Wǒ néng yòng........................... ma?**

d **Nǐ néng bù néng gěi wǒ jiào yī liàng...................**

e **Qǐng gěi wǒ ....**

3 Say these dates in Chinese:

a Christmas Day   b New Year's Eve
c New Year's Day   d St. Valentine's Day

Now say today's date, including the day of the week and the year, and then say your date of birth.

now you're talking!

1   **2•50** Imagine you're in a hotel in Nanjing, looking for a room for just one night.

- **Huānyíng guānglín. Wǒ néng bāngzhù nǐ ma?** *Can I help you?*
- ◆ Ask if they have a room available.
- **Shuāngrén jiān háishi liǎngrén jiān?**
- ◆ You want a twin room, with a bathroom.
- **Nǐ yào zhù jǐ wǎn?**
- ◆ Answer his question.
- **Yǒu kòng fángjiān.**
- ◆ Ask how much the room costs.
- **Liù bǎi yuán.**
- ◆ Ask if breakfast is included.
- **Bāo zǎocān.**

2   **2•51** Now take the part of Debbie Marshall, arriving at the Dōngfāng Fàndiàn, where she has a room booked for a week.

- Greet the man at reception and say you've got a reservation.
- ◆ **Nín guì xìng?**
- Answer his question.
- ◆ **Dānrén jiān dài kōngtiáo. Sān ge wǎnshang.**
- That's not right. Tell him how long you're staying.
- ◆ **Qǐng shāo děng. Hǎo - yī ge xīngqī. Dào sānyuè liù hào. Qǐng gěi wǒ nínde hùzhào.**
- Hand your passport to him. Say here it is. Now ask if you can pay by credit card.
- ◆ **Dāngrán kěyǐ.**

quiz

1 What do you hand over if you're asked for your **hùzhào**?

2 Which of these is the odd one out? **liǎngrén, Měiguórén, shuāngrén, dānrén**.

3 How do you ask if breakfast is included?

4 Which month comes before **bāyuè**? Which follows it?

5 What is a **chūzūchē**?

6 If you wanted a wake-up call at 7 o'clock, would you say **Nǐ néng bù néng liù diǎn jiào xǐng wǒ?** or **Nǐ néng bù néng qī diǎn jiào xǐng wǒ?**

7 How do you think you say *She wants to stay for 2 weeks* in Chinese?

8 Given that **xǐyīfáng** is a laundry service, how do you ask a) if there's a laundry service, b) if you can use it?

Now check whether you can ...

- say you've booked a room
- ask if there's a room available
- specify whether you want a single, double or twin, with bathroom/air-conditioning
- say how long you want accommodation for, giving precise dates
- ask if you can do something, e.g. pay by credit card
- ask someone else to do something for you

Whenever you take part in a conversation, imagine yourself in that particular situation. What would you expect to hear if you were in a hotel in an English-speaking country, for example? This will help you anticipate what people are going to say – which makes it easier for you to focus and understand what's being said.

Huǒchē jǐ diǎn kāi?

saying where you're going

asking about public transport

finding out train times

... and buying tickets

Zài Zhōngguó ...

chē can refer to anything with wheels if the context makes it clear what's being talked about. If not, you need the full version, ending in chē: qìchē *car/vehicle*, gōnggòng qìchē *bus*, diànchē *tram*, chūzūchē *taxi*, zìxíngchē *bicycle*, mótuōchē *motorbike*, huǒchē *train*.

In big towns public transport is cheap and frequent, and practically all China's main towns and cities are linked by China Rail – 中国铁路 Zhōngguó Tiělù – one of the biggest and busiest networks in the world. Its trains include P-category pǔtōng lièchē *ordinary trains*, K-category pǔkuài lièchē *fast ordinary trains*, T-category tèkuài lièchē *express fast trains*, Z-category zhídá tèkuài *express (non-stop) fast trains* and the prestige D-category dònglì chēzǔ *high-speed trains*. Services are numbered, with the category shown by a prefix, e.g. Z19, D31.

Saying where you're going

1   2•52 Listen to the key language:

Wǒ qù/Wǒ yào qù …	I'm going to/I want to go to …
(Nǐ kěyǐ) zuò dìtiě/chūzūchē.	(You can) take the underground/ a taxi.
… huòzhě gōnggòng qìchē.	… or a bus.
Nǐ shénme shíhòu qù?	When are you going?
jīntiān/míngtiān	today/tomorrow

2   2•53 A visitor to Beijing is asking the hotel receptionist for advice on going to Tiān'ānmén Square. Listen and tick the vehicles you hear mentioned. When does he want to go?

 ....
 ....
 ....

Zài Zhōngwén lǐ …

or is huòzhě in a statement and háishi in a question: Nǐ kěyǐ zuò chūzūchē huòzhě gōnggòng qìchē *You can take a taxi or a bus*; Nǐ zuò chūzūchē háishi gōnggòng qìchē? *Are you taking a taxi or a bus?*

---

3   2•54 Another visitor wants to explore the town centre. Listen and fill the gaps in the conversation with the words from the box. **Dìtú** is a *map*.

huòzhě	háishi
shénme shíhou	
qù	yǒu

- ● Wǒ yào .... shì zhōngxīn.
- ◆ Nǐ .... qù? Jīntiān .... míngtiān?
- ● Míngtiān.
- ◆ Nǐ kěyǐ zuò dìtiě .... chūzūchē.
- ● Hǎo. Nǐ .... dìtú ma?
- ◆ Gěi nǐ.

Asking about public transport

1   2•55 Listen to the key language:

Yǒu .... (gōnggòng qì)chē ma?	Is there a bus to …?
Zhè ge chē qù … ma?	Does this bus go to …?
Zhè ge chē <u>shénme shíhou</u> kāi?	<u>When</u> does this bus leave?
Zuò jǐ lù chē qù …?	Which number bus goes to …?
Duō jiǔ néng dào?	How long does it take to get there?

Zài Zhōngwén lǐ …

zhōng *clock*, diǎn (zhōng) *o'clock* and fēn(zhōng) *minute* are the key words when talking about time: wǔ diǎn (zhōng) *5 o'clock*, wǔ fēnzhōng *5 minutes*. Wǔ fēnzhōng yǐhòu means *in 5 minutes' time*, and měi wǔ fēnzhōng is *every 5 minutes*.

Xiǎoshí means *one hour*, and the number word is ge: liǎng ge xiǎoshí *two hours*; měi xiǎoshí *every hour*, měi bàn xiǎoshí *every half an hour*.

2   2•56 Read the names of landmarks found in and around Beijing, listen to passengers making enquiries at **gōnggòng qìchē zǒngzhàn** *the bus station*, and make a note of the information given. Listen out for **yāo**, which is used instead of **yī** *one* in a series of numbers.

● 北海公园 **Běihǎi Gōngyuán** *Beihai Park* ....

● 故宫 **Gù gōng** *The Forbidden City* ....

● 雍和宫 **Yōnghégōng** *The Lama Temple* ....

● 天安门 **Tiān'ānmén** *Tiananmen Square* ....

● 长城 **Chángchéng** *The Great Wall* ....

● 颐和园 **Yíhéyuán** *The Summer Palace* ....

3   Now practise using the key questions in 1 above with the various places, e.g. ask if there's a bus to Tiananmen Square, which number bus goes to the Summer Palace?

Finding out train times

1 2•57 Listen to the key language:

Jǐ diǎn?	What time?
Huǒchē jǐ diǎn kāi?	What time does the train leave?
Qù Xī'ān de huǒchē jǐ diǎn kāi?	What time does the Xī'an train leave?
<u>**Xià yī tàng/bān**</u> **qù Xī'ān de huǒchē jǐ diǎn kāi?**	What time is the <u>next</u> train to Xī'an?
Huǒchē jǐ diǎn dào Xī'ān?	What time does the train arrive in Xī'an?

Zài Zhōngwén lǐ ...

when saying what time things occur, *at* is not translated:

(at) 3.00 **sān diǎn**	(at) 3.20 **sān diǎn èrshí (fēn)**
(at) 3.05 **sān diǎn líng wǔ**	(at) 3.45 **sān diǎn sìshíwǔ (fēn)**

As in English, there are alternatives, e.g. 3.30 can be either **sān diǎn sānshí** or **sān diǎn bàn** *half past three*. *A quarter past* is **yī kè** and *a quarter to* is **chà yī kè**.

The 24-hour clock is not generally used in everyday speech; **zǎoshang, xiàwǔ** etc. are added when clarification is needed: **Zǎoshang liù diǎn bàn** 6.30 *in the morning*.

---

2 2•58 Listen to people in Beijing station enquiring about trains and fill in the departure time. Note that 2 is **liǎng**, not **èr**, when referring to time.

常州 **Chángzhōu** ....   沈阳 **Shěnyáng** ....
南京 **Nánjīng** ....   秦皇岛 **Qínhuángdǎo** ....
上海 **Shànghǎi** ....

3 2•59 Listen to another passenger then decide whether the following are true or false.

	True	False
a There's a train to Xī'an in half an hour.		
b It leaves at 7.03.		
c It arrives in Xī'an at 6.48am.		

...and buying tickets

4   2•60 Listen to the key language:

Yǒu piào ma?	Are there tickets available?
Wǒ yào mǎi	I want to buy
... **yī zhāng piào/liǎng zhāng piào**	... 1 ticket/2 tickets
... **yī zhāng qù Sūzhōu de piào**	... 1 ticket to Suzhou
... **yī zhāng dānchéng/wǎngfǎn piào**	... 1 single/return ticket
... **yī zhāng ruǎnzuò/yìngwò piào**	...1 soft seat/hard sleeper ticket

5   2•61 Olivia Lam is travelling from Shanghai to Suzhou with friends. In the ticket office, she's asked **Nǐmen yào mǎi jǐ zhāng piào?** *How many tickets do you want?* Listen, then fill the gaps in this summary of what took place.

**Lam xiǎojie mǎi .... zhāng .... piào.
Tā yào ruǎnzuò piào.**

6   2•62 Listen to the next passenger then provide the travel information. You'll hear the train number **Z shísān cì** *Z13*. **Cì** is used for train numbers, whereas **lù** is used for buses.

destination	dep. time	arr. time ....
ticket	seat	¥ ....

售票处
Shòupiàochù
ticket office

put it all together

1   Match the times to the clocks.

1 `02.25`   2 `10.05`   3 `08.35`

4 `01.15`   5 `03.50`   6 `05.10`

a Yī diǎn shíwǔ   b bā diǎn sānshíwǔ
c liǎng diǎn èrshíwǔ   d shí diǎn líng wǔ
e wǔ diǎn shí fēn   f sān diǎn wǔshí

2   Say these times in Chinese, using *quarter/half* where
    appropriate. You might need to refer to page 82.

a 7.30am   b 6.23pm
c 12.15pm   d 10.40am
e 4.05pm   f 4.45am

3   Which is the odd one out and why?

a **zǎoshang , zǎocān, zhōngwǔ, wǎnshang, shàngwǔ**
b **zìxíngchē, tèkuàichē, pǔtōngchē, pǔkuàichē, huǒchē**
c **míngtiān, xiànzài, jīntiān, jīnwǎn, píngguǒ**
d **hùzhào, ruǎnzuò, yìngzuò, ruǎnwò, yìngwò**
e **xiǎoshí, diǎn, fēn, zhōng, piào**

4   Rearrange the words to discover three questions related to
    travel. What do they mean?

a gōnggòng qìchē   ma   Chángchéng   yǒu

   de   qù

b Běijīng   qù   nǐ   shénme shíhou

c huǒchē   jǐ diǎn   Nánjīng de   kāi

   xià yī tàng   qù

now you're talking!

1 **2•63** You're with a friend at a **gōnggòng qìchē zhàn** in Beijing, on your way to the **Yíhéyuán** *Summer Palace*.

- Ask the woman in the office if there's a bus to the Summer Palace.
◆ **Yǒu. Qīshíbā lù chē. Měi shí fēnzhōng yī tàng.**
- Tell your friend what number bus it is and how often they go. Now find out how long it takes to get there.
◆ **Èrshíwǔ fēnzhōng.**
- Ask how much a ticket costs.
◆ **Shíliù yuán.**
- Say you want to buy two tickets.
◆ **Gěi nǐ.**
- Thank her.
◆ **Bú xiè.**

2 **2•64** Now you're off to Xī'an by train on your own.

- Ask the man in the ticket office what time the next train leaves.
◆ **Liù diǎn sìshíwǔ fēn.**
- Find out what time the train arrives in Xī'an.
◆ **Zǎoshang qī diǎn líng wǔ.**
- Say you'd like a ticket.
◆ **Dānchéng háishi wǎngfǎn?**
- You want a single.
◆ **Nǐ yào ruǎnzuò piào ma?**
- It's a long journey. Say you want a soft sleeper and ask the price.
◆ **Liùshí'èr yuán. Gěi nǐ. Yí lù píng ān.** *Bon voyage!*

quiz

1. Is **jiǔ diǎn chā yī kè** 9.15 or 8.45? What would 9.30 be?
2. What would you be waiting for at a **gōnggòng qìchē zhàn**?
3. Why would you go to a **shòupiàochù**?
4. Would you use **háishi** or **huòzhě** to mean or in a question?
5. What kind of train is a **tèkuài lièchē**? What prefixes the train number?
6. Is a **yìngzuò** or a **ruǎnwò** likely to be more comfortable? What is **zhàn piào**?
7. What's the difference between **měi bàn xiǎoshí** and **bàn xiǎoshí yǐhòu**?
8. Given that **guānmén** means *to close*, how would you ask what time the bank closes?

Now check whether you can ...

- say where you're going/want to go
- ask if there's a bus going to a particular place
- find out when it leaves
- ask how long it takes to get to a place
- ask what time a train departs and arrives
- understand the time of day
- buy a ticket, single or return, for various seats

On the internet there's a wealth of information about **Zhōngguó Tiělù** *China Rail*, including detail of timetables, ticket prices, etc. Using it to plan a hypothetical journey will bring to life what you've just learnt – work out what questions you'd need to ask to buy tickets for particular seats, and to find out what time trains leave and what time they arrive at their destination. **Yí lù píng ān!**

Mànmàn chī

choosing a place to eat

understanding what's on the menu

ordering a meal

expressing appreciation

Zài Zhōngguó ...

most eating places serve breakfast, lunch and dinner; in-between some also serve **diǎnxīn** *snacks* (**dímsum** in Cantonese). **Chá** is traditionally served with meals, but soft drinks, **píjiǔ** and **pútáojiǔ** are also popular now.

There are eight major regional cuisines: **yuècài** *Cantonese/Guangdong* (exotic ingredients, light, mild), **lǔcài** *Shandong* (seafood, peanuts, shallots/garlic seasoning), **mǐncài** *Fujian* (seafood, tasty, pickled ingredients) **jiāngsūcài** *Jiangsu* (fish/crustaceans, delicate, sweet), **zhècài** *Zhejiang* (smooth, mellow), **huīcài** *Anhui* (slow-cooked braised dishes). **chuāncài** *Sichuan/Szechuan* and **xiāngcài** *Hunan* make much use of chilli, garlic, ginger and pepper and can be very **là** *hot/spicy*.

Choosing a place to eat

1   2•65 Listen to the key language:

Wǒmen wǎnshang chī shénme?	What shall we eat tonight?
Wǒmen chī ..., hǎo bù hǎo?	What if we eat ...?
Wǒ (bù) xǐhuan ...	I (don't) like ...
Wǒ hěn xǐhuan	I really like ...
Wǒ gèng xǐhuan ...	I prefer ...
Hǎo zhǔyi	Good idea

2   2•66 Listen to Haijiao and some friends discussing where to eat, and tick the key phrases as you hear them. Do they decide on one of these or on **jiǎozi** *dumplings*?

chuāncài	**huīcài**	**lǔcài**	**mǐncài**
jiāngsūcài	**xiāngcài**	**yuècài**	**zhècài**

Zài Zhōngwén lǐ ...

hěn means *very* with adjectives and *very much/really* with adverbs:

Chuāncài hěn là. *Sichuan food is <u>very</u> spicy.*

Wǒ hěn xǐhuān chuāncài. *I like Sichuan food <u>very much</u>.*

---

3   2•67 As they enter the restaurant, they're asked **Nǐmen jǐ wèi?** *How many of you are there? Lit. You how many people?* The MW **wèi** is used instead of the standard **ge** to show extra politeness to customers in shops and restaurants.

Listen as they and another party are greeted, and note how many people there are in each group: **a** .... **wèi**   **b** .... **wèi**

4   2•68 Listen as they're given the **càidān** *menu* and asked what they want to drink **Nǐmen xiǎng hē shénme?** Which of these do they choose?

píjiǔ	**hóng pútáojiǔ**	**chá**	**mǐjiǔ** *rice wine*
	bái pútáojiǔ	**kuàngquán shuǐ**	

Understanding what's on the menu

1 Have a look at the following:

---

yú *fish* **hǎixiān** *seafood* **xiā** *shrimp* **dàxiā** *prawns* **lóngxiā** *lobster*
ròu *meat* **niúròu** *beef* **zhūròu** *pork* **yángròu** *lamb*
páigǔ *spare ribs* **jī(ròu)** *chicken* **jīdàn** *eggs* **yā** *duck* **dòufu** *tofu*

shícài/qīngcài *seasonal/green vegetables* **bōcài** *spinach*
báicài *Chinese leaves* **jièlán** *Chinese broccoli*
dòuyá *beansprouts* **xīhóngshì** *tomato* **mógu** *mushroom*
cōng *onion* **suàn** *garlic*

mǐfàn *rice* **bái (mǐ)fàn** *boiled (lit. white) rice* **dàn chǎo fàn** *egg-fried rice* **miàn(tiáo)** *noodles* **bāozi** *steamed bun* **jiǎozi** *dumplings*

jiān *fried* **zhá** *deep fried* **chǎo** *stir fried/sautéed* **kǎo** *roasted*
lǔshuǐ *marinated* **qīngzhēng** *steamed* **gālí** *curry* **tángcù** *sweet and sour lit. sugar vinegar* **suānlà** *hot and sour lit. sour hot*

---

2 Now work out what these dishes are.

汤 **Tāng** *Soups*

鱼汤 **yú tāng**　　　　　　　酸辣汤 **suānlà tāng**

主食 **Zhǔshí** *Staple carbohydrates*

白米饭 **bái mǐfàn**　　　　　　蛋炒饭 **dàn chǎofàn**
炒面 **chǎomiàn**

主菜 **Zhǔcài** *Main courses*

糖醋鸡 **tángcù jī**　　　　　　炒羊肉 **chǎo yángròu**
北京烤鸭 **Běijīng kǎoyā**　　　咖哩牛肉 **gālí niúròu**
卤水豆腐 **lǔshuǐ dòufu**　　　　糖醋排骨 **tángcù páigǔ**
时菜 **shícài**　　　　　　　　　炒芥兰蘑菇 **chǎo jièlán mógu**

Ordering a meal

1 **2•69** Listen to the key language:

Qǐng lái ...	Please bring ...
... yī ge gālí jīròu	... 1 chicken curry
... yī zhī kǎoyā	... 1 roast duck
... yī wǎn mǐfàn	... 1 bowl of rice
Wǒmen dōu yào ...	We both/all want ...
... là bú là?	Is the ... spicy?

2 **2•70** First work out what these two questions mean, then listen as Haijiao starts ordering and jot down his order. You'll hear **nàme** *in that case/then so.*

Zhǔcài yào shénme?
Zhǔshí yào shénme?

> **Nǐmen diǎn cài ma?**
> *Are you ready to order?*

3 **2•71** Haijiao's Australian friend Amanda talks to the waitress about an item on the menu. Before listening, read their conversation and work out what **chīsù** means. What does she order?

- Wǒ bù chī ròu – wǒ chīsù. Zhè ge cài yǒu méi yǒu ròu?
- ◆ Yǒu. Nín chī dàn ma?
- Bù chī dàn. Lǔshuǐ dòufu là bú là?
- ◆ Bú là, bú là.
- Nàme, qǐng lái yī ge lǔshuǐ dòufu, xièxie.

Zài Zhōngguó ...

at the start of a meal, you might be told **Mànmàn chī** which literally means *Slowly slowly eat*, in other words, *Take your time and enjoy your meal.* An alternative is **Màn yòng**. **Gān bēi** traditionally expects you to empty your glass, although it's increasingly used simply as *Cheers.*

---

4 **2•72** As the meal is served, Haijiao calls the **fúwùyuán** (the word for both *waiter* and *waitress*). What does he order to drink? He asks for something else – **zái lài** *as well.* Is it:

chāzi **kuàizi** or **sháozi**?

Expressing appreciation

1   2•73 Listen to the key language:

Gòu ma?	Is that enough?
Gòu le.	That's enough.
Nǐ chī bǎo le ma?	Are you full?
Wǒ chī bǎo le.	I'm full.
Fàncài hěn hǎochī.	The food is/was delicious.
Qǐng jiézhàng/mǎidān.	The bill, please.

2   2•74 The waitress asks **Hái yào biéde ma?** *Anything else?* and Haijiao checks with his friends. Listen and make a note of how they reply.

Tíng Huá ……………………………………………………

Jiàn Zhōng ……………………………………………………

Amanda ……………………………………………………

Zài Zhōngwén lǐ ...

le, which doesn't translate into English, has several functions, including:

- showing a change of state: **wǒ chī bǎo le** *I'm full* (whereas I wasn't before);
- meaning *extremely*, when used with **tài** and an adjective: **tài hǎo le** *extremely good*. Another way of saying *extremely* is **fēicháng**.

G12

---

3   2•75 The waitress then asks if they enjoyed their meal **Fàncài zěnmeyàng?** Listen as they reply and add the compliments.

- **Fàncài zěnmeyàng?**
- ◆ ………………………… **xièxie.**
- **Kǎoyā …………………………, …………………………!**
- ◆ **Qǐng jiézhàng.**
- **Qǐng shāo děng. Gěi nín.**
- ◆ **Jīntiān wǒ qǐngkè.** *Today it's my treat.*
- **Xièxie.**
- ◆ **Zàijiàn!**

put it all together

1 Put these in the order you're most likely to hear them in a restaurant.

  a Zhǔshí yào shénme?   b Xièxie. Zàijiàn!
  c Nǐmen xiǎng hē shénme?   d Zhǔcài yào shénme?
  e Zhè shì zhàngdān.   f Fàncài zěnmeyàng?
  g Qǐng wèn, nǐmen jǐ wèi?   h Zhè shì càidān.

2 Which of these would you use

wǒ bù chī yú

wǒ hěn xǐhuan yú

yú tài hǎo le

wǒ gèng xǐhuan yú

zhè ge yú là ma

wǒ bù xǐhuan yú

  a if you don't like fish?   b to say you don't eat fish?
  c to say you prefer fish?   d when you really like fish?
  e when the fish is extremely good?   f to ask if this fish is spicy?

3 What are these dishes?

  a hǎixiān tāng   b niúròu tāng
  c tángcù zhūròu   d chǎo qīngcài dòufu
  e gālí yángròu   f zhá dàxiā
  g xīhóngshì jīdàn tāng   h jiān dàn

4 In Chinese, how would you

  a say you like Cantonese food?
  b ask someone if he likes rice wine?
  c say you prefer beer?
  d say you both really like **Zhōngcān** Chinese food?

1 **2•76** Imagine you're in a restaurant in Beijing with a friend who doesn't speak Chinese. You're greeted by the waitress.

- **Huānyíng guānglín. Qǐng wèn, jǐ wèi.**
- Say there are two of you.
- **Qǐng zuò. Nǐmen yào hē shénme?**
- Say you'll both drink tea please.
- **Zhè shì càidān.**
- Thank her.

She returns a few minutes later.
- **Nǐmen diǎncài ma?**
- Ask for one stir-fried beef and a Beijing roast duck.
- **Zhǔshí yào shénme?**
- Order a bowl of boiled rice and a bowl of noodles.
- **Nǐmen yào kuàizi háishi chāzi?**
- She's asking if you want chopsticks or forks. Go for the chopsticks.

When she brings the food ...
- **Gěi nín – yī ge chǎo niúròu hé yī zhī kǎoyā, mǐfàn, miàntiáo. Hái yào biéde ma?**
- Ask her to bring two bottles of beer.
- **Hǎo. Mànmàn chī.**

When you've finished ...
- **Fàncài zěnmeyàng?**
- Say the food was delicious.
  Now ask for the bill.
- **Qǐng shāo děng.**

quiz

1 Going into a restaurant, how would you say there are four of you?

2 Would **hóngshāo yángròu** be suitable for a vegetarian?

3 How do you attract the attention of the waiter or waitress?

4 Which is the odd one out? **dòuyá, dàxiā, hǎixiān, yú, lóngxiā.**

5 If **Zhōngcān** is *Chinese food*, what do you think **Xīcān** is?

6. What's the difference between a) **Zhǔshí yào shénme?** and b) **Zhǔshí yǒu shénme?**

7 How would you find out if **yú xiāng niúròu** is spicy?

8 Given that nuts are **guǒrén**, how would you ask if **gālí niúroù** has nuts in it?

Now check whether you can ...

- understand the Chinese for basic menu items
- order a meal, main course and staple, and a drink
- say what you like, don't like and prefer
- pay a compliment on the food
- ask for the bill
- offer to pay for the meal

Now get ready for the final Checkpoint, which covers the whole of **Talk Mandarin Chinese**, with a bit of revision. Listen to the conversations again, test your knowledge of the key language by covering up the English and the Chinese in turn, and use the quizzes and checklists at the end of each unit to assess how much you remember.

Checkpoint 3

Imagine you've just arrived in China on holiday ...

1 It's Sunday. Tired and thirsty, you arrive at Beijing's rail station, and look for the nearest bar. Which of these questions would you ask?

  a Duìbuqǐ, yǒu cānguǎn ma?
  b Duìbuqǐ, jiǔbā jīntiān kāimén ma?
  c Duìbuqǐ, zuìjìn de jiǔbā zài nǎr?
  d Duìbuqǐ, shìchǎng zài nǎr?

2 Having found a bar, you order a drink.

  ● Nín hǎo. Nín hē shénme?
  ◆ A bottle of beer ....
  ● Xiǎo de háishi dà de?
  ◆ A large one please. ....
  ● How much is it? ....
  ◆ Èrshísì yuán.

Note down in words how much change you'd expect from a 100 **yuán** note.

3 After your drink, how would you ask the waiter   **Qǐng wèn ...**

  a where the toilet is?
  b if there's an internet café nearby?
  c whether the post office is open today?
  d how to get to the Xin Gang Wan Hotel?

4 **2•77** Listen to his reply to the last question and make a note in English of the directions you're given.

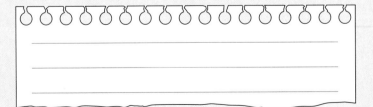

5   Before leaving the station, you want to find out what time there's a train for Dàlián on Thursday, what time it arrives and how much a return ticket costs. For each question, choose the correct options.

a   Xīngqīyī/xīngqīsì qù Dàlián de huǒchē/chūzūchē jǐ diǎn kāi?

b   Huǒchē jǐ diǎn zài/dào Dàlián?

c   Duōshao qián yī zhāng wǎngfǎn/dānchéng piào?

6   You've already booked an en suite room at the Xin Gang Wan Hotel for a week. At reception which of the following would you say?

a   Wǒ yùdìng le sān wǎnshang dānrén jiān dài yùshì.
b   Wǒ xiǎng yào dài kōngtiáo de fángjiān, cóng jīntiān dào xīngqīsì.
c   Yǒu kòng dānrén jiān dài yùshì qī ge wǎnshang ma?
d   Wǒ yùdìng le yī ge xīngqī de dānrén jiān dài yùshì.

7   2•78 Listen to the receptionist's reply. Make a note in English of the two things she asks you, your room number and where the lift is.

a   ....
b   ....
c   ....
d   ....

8   2•79 In the evening you go looking for a birthday present for your sister. Listen to the audio and take part in a conversation in a shop selling **pí** leather. You'll need to be able to say:

● I want to buy a **shǒutíbāo** handbag.
● It's too big.
● Can I have a look at that one?
● I really like it.
● How much is it?
● It's too expensive.
● How about 800 yuan?
● Can I pay by credit card?

9 Later in the hotel bar, you get talking to Tanaka Keiko, who's Japanese, from Tokyo.

How would she answer these questions?

a **Nǐ jiào shénme?**
b **Nǐ shì bú shì Zhōngguórén?**

10 2•80 What questions would you need to have asked Keiko if these are her replies?

a ....
● **Wǒ zhù zài Dōngjīng.**

b ....
● **Wǒ shì gōngchéngshī.**

c ....
● **Wǒ jiéhūn le.**

d ....
● **Wǒ yǒu yī ge érzi.**

e ....
● **Tā jiǔ suì.**

f ....
● **Wǒ huì shuō yìdiǎn Yīngwén. Nǐ Zhōngwén shuō de zhēn hǎo!**

g ....
● **Xǐhuan – wǒ hěn xǐhuan Běijīng cài. Fēicháng hǎo!**

She now asks you about yourself. Listen to the audio and answer her.

11 2•81 Listen to Keiko's plans for the week and note in the diary when she'll be in Beijing, Dalian and Jinzhou and when she's returning to Japan. As in English, the present tense of verbs is used for the future when the context makes it clear when things are happening.

dāi *to stay*
dào *to arrive*
zhídào *until*

Mon		**Fri**	
....		....	
Tues		**Sat**	
....		....	
Wed		**Sun**	
....		....	
Thur			
....			

12 Later, Keiko helps you to decipher the menu in the hotel restaurant. First have a look at these characters for ingredients you know.

鱼 **yú**   肉 **ròu**

大虾 **dàxiā**   羊肉 **yángròu**

鸡 **jī**   牛肉 **niúròu**

鸭 **yā**   猪肉 **zhūròu**

豆腐 **dòufu**

Now use the above ingredients as the key to match the following.

a	鱼香牛肉	1	**Běijīng kǎoyā** *Beijing roast duck*
b	油焖大虾	2	**dòufu shāo yú** *fried fish with tofu*
c	豆腐烧鱼	3	**qīngzhēng quánjī** *steamed whole chicken*
d	北京烤鸭	4	**yú xiāng niúròu** *Yu-Shiang spicy garlic beef*
e	清蒸全鸡	5	**yóumèn dàxiā** *braised prawns*

Finally, identify the main ingredient of these dishes (Pinyin and English on page 89).

f 牛肉炖土豆 ....

g 啤酒鸡 ....

h 烤羊腿 ....

i 野菌烧豆腐 ....

j 豆腐烧鱼 ....

k 砂锅鱼头 ....

l 猪肉炖粉条 ....

m 干锅鸡 ....

n 西湖醋鱼 ....

o 涮羊肉 ....

Liǎobuqǐ *Congratulations.* You've reached the end of **Talk Mandarin Chinese**. Be prepared to hear **Nǐ Zhōngwén shuō de zhēn hǎo** and to reply modestly **Nǎli nǎli!**

transcripts and answers

This section contains the scripts of all the **Talk Mandarin Chinese** conversations. Answers which consist of words/phrases from the conversations are in bold type; other answers are given separately.

Unit 1

Pages 8-9 Saying hello and goodbye

2 ● Nǐ hǎo.
  ◆ Nǐ hǎo.
  ● Luó Píng, nǐ hǎo ma?
  ◆ **Hěn hǎo**, xièxie.
  She's very well.

3 ● Nǐ hǎo.
  ◆ Nín hǎo.
  ● Nǐ hǎo ma?
  ◆ Wǒ hěn hǎo, xièxie.
  ● Nǐmen hǎo.
  ◆ Nǐ hǎo.
  ● Nǐmen hǎo ma?
  ◆ Wǒmen hěn hǎo, xièxie.
  ● Wáng Wěiléi, nǐ hǎo ma?
  ◆ Mǎmǎhūhū. Nǐ ne?
  ● Hěn hǎo, xièxie.
  She greets a single person first. You hear xièxie 3 times.

4 ● Fàn Yǒng, **zǎoshang hǎo**.
  ◆ Luó Píng, **zǎoshang hǎo**.
  ● Wú Lán, **nǐ hǎo**.
  ◆ Nǐ hǎo.
  ● Lǐ xiānsheng, **wǎnshang hǎo**.
  ◆ Wǎnshang hǎo.
  ● Wáng Yuányuan, **nǐ hǎo**.
  ◆ Luó Píng, nǐ hǎo.
  ● Chén Jiàntāo, **zǎoshang hǎo**.
  ◆ Zǎoshang hǎo.

6 ● Lǐ xiānsheng, **míngtiān jiàn**.
  ◆ Zhào Mǐn, **huítóu jiàn**.
  ● Chén tàitai, **zàijiàn**.
  ◆ Lǐ Yǒng, **wǎn'ān. Míngtiān jiàn**.
  ● Zhào Wěiléi, **wǎnshang jiàn**.

7 ● Zàijiàn, zàijiàn.
  ◆ Zàijiàn, Tíngting, **míngtiān jiàn**.
  ● Léilei, **wǎnshang jiàn**.

  Tíngting: **míngtiān jiàn** *tomorrow*;
  Léilei: **wǎnshang jiàn** *this evening*.

8 bǎi; è; sī; wō; wǔ; yù
  chá; chē; běi; xī; wò; lù; yǔ

Pages 10-11 Introducing yourself and getting to know people

2 ● Duìbuqǐ, nín shì Chén xiānsheng ma?
  ◆ Wǒ bú shì.
  ● Nín shì Chén xiānsheng ma?
  ◆ Wǒ bú shì.
  ● Duìbuqǐ, nín shì Chén xiānsheng ma?
  ◆ Shìde, wǒ shì.

3 ● Nǐ shì Gāo Zǐxiáng xiānsheng ma?
  ◆ Bú shì, wǒ shì **Gāo Zhìqiáng**.

4 ● Nǐ shì Zhōng xiǎojie ma?
  ◆ Wǒ bú shì.
  ● Wǒ shì + *your name*.

6 ● **Wǒ jiào** Zhào Zhōuzhou.
  ◆ Hěn gāoxìng rènshi nǐ.

7 ● Nǐ hǎo. Nǐ xìng shénme? Nǐ shì Wáng xiānsheng ma?
  ◆ Bú shì. Wǒ xìng **Huáng**. Wǒ jiào **Huáng Xuě**.
  ● Nín hǎo, Huáng xiānsheng, hěn gāoxìng rènshi nín.
  ◆ Wǒ yě hěn gāoxìng rènshi nǐ.

8 ● **Zǎoshang** hǎo. **Nín** shì Wáng Hǎiqìng xiānsheng **ma**?
  ◆ Shì, **wǒ** shì.
  ● Wǒ **shì** Lǐ Xiǎoyuè. **Hěn** gāoxìng rènshi nín.

Page 12 Put it all together

1 *a* Nǐ jiào shénme?; *b* Nǐ hǎo; *c* Wǒ jiào; *d* Duìbuqǐ; *e* Wǎnshang hǎo; *f* Wǒ bú shì; *g* Wǎn'ān; *h* Wǒ hěn hǎo,

xièxie; *i* Hěn gāoxìng rènshi nǐ.
Nǐ hǎo ma? *(How are you?) is left over.*

2 *1* Nǐ hǎo.
2 Zǎoshang hǎo.
3 Nǐmen hǎo.
4 Zàijiàn.

Page 13 Now you're talking!

1 • **Nǐ hǎo.**
  ◆ Zǎoshang hǎo. Nǐ xìng shénme?
  • **Wǒ xìng Newman.**
  ◆ Shì Jake Newman xiānsheng ma?
  • **Shìde, wǒ shì Jake Newman. Duìbuqǐ, tā shì Gǒng Lì ma?**
  ◆ Shìde, tā shì Gǒng Lì.

2 • Zǎoshang hǎo. Wǒ shì Huáng Nà. Nǐ jiào shénme?
  ◆ **Wǒ shì Jake Newman.**
  • Hěn gāoxìng rènshi nǐ.
  ◆ **Hěn gāoxìng rènshi nǐ, Huáng Nà.**
  • **Huáng Nà, zàijiàn.**
  ◆ Míngtiān jiàn.

3 • Gāo Wénpíng, wǎnshang hǎo.
  ◆ **Wǎnshang hǎo.**
  • Nǐ hǎo ma?
  ◆ **Mǎmǎhūhū. Nǐ ne?**
  • Wǒ hěn hǎo, xièxie.

Page 14 Quiz

1 *1* when greeting more than one person; *2* **hěn hǎo**, **xièxie**, **mǎmǎhūhū**; *3* **wǎnshang hǎo** *good evening*, **wǎnshang jiàn** *see you this evening*, **míngtiān wǎnshang** *tomorrow evening*; *4* what his/her name is; *5* when you first meet somebody; *6* **shì/shìde** *yes*, **bú shì** *no*; *7* a married woman; *8* **xīngqīliù jiàn**.

Unit 2

Pages 16 & 17 Talking about nationality and where you come from

2 • Duìbuqǐ, nǐ shì nǎ guó rén?
  ◆ Wǒ shì Xīnxīlánrén.

• Nǐ shì nǎ guó rén?
◆ Wǒ shì Yīngguórén.
• Duìbuqǐ, nǐ shì Měiguórén ma?
◆ Bú shì, wǒ shì Jiānádàrén.
• Nǐ ne?
◆ Wǒ shì Yīngguórén.
• Nǐ shì nǎ guó rén?
◆ Wǒ shì Xīnxīlánrén.

1 Xīnxīlánrén; 2 Yīngguórén; 3 Jiānádàrén; 4 Yīngguórén; 5 Xīnxīlánrén

3 Zhōngguó Zhōngguórén; Hánguó Hánguórén; Rìběn Rìběnrén; Yīnggélán Yīnggélánrén; Sūgélán Sūgélánrén; Wēi'ěrshì Wēi'ěrshìrén; Àodàliyà Àodàliyàrén; Ài'ěrlán Ài'ěrlánrén.

6 • Nǐ cóng nǎr lái? **Wǒ cóng Ài'ěrlán lái.**
  ◆ Nǐ ne? **Wǒ shì Àodàliyàrén, wǒ cóng Xīní lái.**
  • Ní yě shì Àodàliyàrén ma? **Bú shì, wǒ cóng Lúndūn lái.**
  ◆ Nǐ cóng nǎr lái? **Wǒ cóng Měiguó lái, cóng Niǔyuē lái.**
  • Ní shì běndìrén ma? **Shìde, wǒ shì Shànghǎirén.**
  ◆ Ní yě shì Shànghǎirén ma? **Bù. Wǒ shì Nánjīngrén … wǒ cóng Nánjīng lái.**

7 • Nǐ hǎo. Nǐ jiào shénme?
  ◆ Wǒ jiào Hannah.
  • Nǐ cóng nǎr lái?
  ◆ Wǒ shì Yīngguórén – wǒ cóng **Lánkǎisītè** lái.
  • Wǒ jiào Mark … Wǒ jiào Susie.
  ◆ Hěn gāoxìng rènshi nǐmen. Nǐmen cóng nǎr lái?
  • Wǒmen shì Àodàliyàrén – wǒmen cóng **Kānpéilā** lái.

Page 18 Saying what you do for a living

2 • Nǐ zuò shénme gōngzuò?
  ◆ Wǒ shì **dǎoyóu**.
  • Nǐ zuò shénme gōngzuò?

- ◆ Wǒ shì **lǎoshī**.
- ● Xiānsheng, nǐ ne?
- ◆ Wǒ shì **lǜshī**.
- ● Xáojie, nǐ shì xuésheng ma?
- ◆ Bù, wǒ shì **yīshēng**.
- ● Nǐ yě shì yīshēng ma?
- ◆ Bù, wǒ shì **fúwùyuán**.
- ● Nín zuò shénme gōngzuò?
- ◆ Wǒ shì **jìzhě**.
- ● Wǒ shì **gōngchéngshī**.

1 tour guide; 2 teacher; 3 lawyer; 4 doctor; 5 waiter; 6 journalist; 7 engineer.

3 ● Bāo Yúntiān shì yīshēng. Tā zài yīyuàn gōngzuò. Liú Chàng shì gōngchéngshī. Tā zài Shànghǎi yī jiā gōngchǎng gōngzuò. Cài Xuán zài bàngōngshì gōngzuò. Tā shì kuàijìshī.
- ◆ Lín Jiājia ne?
- ● Tā zài dàxué xué Yīngwén.

Bāo Yúntiān: doctor/hospital; Liú Chàng: engineer/factory in Shanghai; Cài Xuán: accountant/office; Lín Jiājia: studies English/University.

Page 19 Giving your phone number

2 bā, sān, wǔ, sì, shí, líng, liù, yī, qī, jiǔ, èr.

4 ● Nǐde diànhuà hàomǎ shì shénme?
- ◆ Wǒde shǒujī hàomǎ shì líng qī qī èr liù líng bā bā líng jiǔ bā. Wǒ jiā de diànhuà hàomǎ shì líng yāo wǔ èr sì bā jiǔ èr wǔ líng líng. Wǒ gōngsī de diànhuà hàomǎ shì líng líng sì sì yāo qī qī èr bā jiǔ èr jiǔ líng jiǔ.

*Home no: 01524 892 500;
Work no: 00 44 1772 892 909.*

Page 20 Put it all together

1 *a* Bù, wǒ shì Sūgélánrén; *b* Shì, wǒ shì Měiguórén; *c* Shì qī bā sān wǔ bā jiǔ; *d* Wǒ shì gōngchéngshī; *e* Bú shì, wǒ shì jìzhě; *f* Wǒ cóng Sūgélán lái.

2 xìng: Yú; guójí: Zhōngguórén; zhíyè: yīshēng; diànhuà hàomǎ: 010 85509166

3 Wǒ **xìng** Liáng. Wǒ **jiào** Liáng Hǎijiāo. Wǒ shì Guǎngzhōurén, wǒ **cóng** Guǎngzhōu **lái**. Wǒ zài **yínháng** gōngzuò, wǒ shì **lǜshī**.

4 Wǒ xìng Huáng. Wǒ jiào Huáng Méilíng. Wǒ shì Zhōngguórén, wǒ cóng Xiānggǎng lái. Wǒ zài bàngōngshì gōngzuò, wǒ shì kuàijìshī.

Wǒ xìng Daniels. Wǒ jiào Rhodri. Wǒ shì Wēi'ěrshìrén, wǒ cóng Bangor lái. Wǒ zài dàxué gōngzuò, wǒ shì lǎoshī.

Page 21 Now you're talking!

1 ● Pí'ěrsūn xiǎojie, nǐ shì Měiguórén ma?
- ◆ **Bú shì**, **wǒ shì Yīngguórén**.
- ● Nǐ cóng nǎr lái?
- ◆ **Wǒ cóng Chester lái.**
- ● Nǐ zuò shénme gōngzuò?
- ◆ **Wǒ shì lǜshī.**

2 ● Duìbuqǐ, dàxué zài nǎr?
- ◆ **Wǒ bú shì běndìrén.**
- ● Nǐ shì Jiānádàrén ma? Yīngguórén? Měiguórén?
- ◆ **Wǒ shì Yīngguórén. Nǐ ne?**
- ● Wǒ shì Yìdàlìrén.
- ◆ **Nǐ shì xuésheng ma?**
- ● Bù, wǒ jiāo Yìdàlìwén. Nǐ ne?
- ◆ **Wǒ yě shì lǎoshī.**
- ● Wǒ jiào Elena Chéng. Nǐ ne?
- ◆ **Wǒ jiào** + your name. **Hěn gāoxìng rènshi nǐ.**
- ● Wó yě hěn gāoxìng rènshi nǐ.

Page 22 Quiz

1 Hong Kong; 2 liù, shí; 3 sān bā wǔ jiǔ bā; 4 your phone number; 5 de; 6 occupation; 7 gōngchéngshī/ gōngchǎng, yīyuàn/yīshēng, dàxué/ xuésheng, dǎoyóu is a tour guide; 8 Fǎguórén, Déguórén.

Unit 3

Pages 24-25 Introducing friends, colleagues and family

2 ● David, zhè shì wǒ tóngshì, Liáng Xiǎoxiá jīnglǐ.
   ◆ Hěn gāoxìng rènshi nǐ, Liáng jīnglǐ. Wǒ **jiào** David. **Zhè** shì **wǒde** míngpiàn.

   *a colleague; b manager; c **jiào** … **Zhè** … **wǒde** …*

3 ● David, zhè shì wǒ **nǚ péngyou** Jiǎng Yuányuan.
   ◆ Hěn gāoxìng rènshi nǐ.
   ● Gěi nǐ jièshào wǒde **péngyou** Huáng Jiànhuán, hé Xǔ Qīng.
   ◆ **Hěn gāoxìng rènshi nǐmen.**

5 ● Wǎnshang hǎo. Zhè shì wǒ **mèimei** Jessica. Jessica, gěi nǐ jièshào wǒde péngyou, Xǔ Qīng.
   ◆ Hěn gāoxìng rènshi nǐ. Zhè shì wǒ zhàngfu, **Lǎo Dèng**.
   ● Hěn gāoxìng rènshi nǐmen.
   ◆ Wǒmen yě hěn gāoxìng rènshi nǐ.
   ● Nǐmen cóng nǎr lái?
   ◆ Wǒmen shì **Xiānggǎngrén**.
   Jessica is younger than David; Xǔ Qīng's husband is Lǎo Dèng; they're from Hong Kong.

6 Zhè shì wǒmen jiā de zhàopiàn. Zhè shì wǒ **àiren** Lǎo Dèng, nà shì wǒde **nǚ'ér** Tíngting. Nà shì wǒ **bàba** hé **māma**. Nà shì wǒ **nǎinai**.
   husband, daughter, mother, father, paternal grandmother.

Pages 26-27 Saying how old you are and talking about your family

2 wǔ, bāshí, shí, shísì, liùshíjiǔ, jiǔshíliù, sì
   40 not mentioned.

3 shísān, shíwǔ, sānshíjiǔ, sìshíbā, shíbā, èrshísì

5 ● Nǐ jǐ suì le?
   ◆ Wǒ **bā** suì.

● Nǐ duō dà le?
◆ Wǒ **èrshíwǔ** suì.
● Nǐ duō dà le?
◆ Wǒ **shíqī** suì.
● Nǐ duō dà suìshu le?
◆ Wǒ **bāshíqī** suì.
8; 25; 17; 87.

7 ● Xiè Zhèngkǎi, nǐ jiéhūn le ma?
   ◆ Wǒ jiéhūn le, wǒ tàitai shì Běijīngrén.
   ● Nǐ yǒu háizi ma?
   ◆ Wǒ yǒu yī ge érzi.
   ● Zhōng Jiéníng, nǐ ne ? Nǐ jiéhūn le ma?
   ◆ Wǒ líhūn le. Wǒ méi yǒu háizi . Nǐ ne, nǐ jiéhūn le ma?
   ● Wǒ jiéhūn le, wǒ yǒu yī ge érzi hé liǎng ge nǚ'ér.
   Zhōng Jiéníng is divorced, the other two are married.

8 *Xiè Zhèngkǎi has a son; Zhōng Jiéníng has no children; Iwan Jones has a son and 2 daughters.*

Page 28 Put it all together

1 *a 1 son; b 2 younger sisters; c 2 daughters; d 12 friends; e 1 older brother; f 2 older sisters.*

2 wǔshí; sìshísān; jiǔshíjiǔ; bāshí; yī bǎi; bāshíbā.

3 *a* Jiànzhōng hé Hǎijiāo yǒu sì ge háizi; *b* Xiǎoqīng yǒu yī ge jiějie; *c* Xiǎoqīng de dìdi dānshēn; *d* Xiǎoqīng yǒu yī ge nǚ'ér; *e* Zìqiáng de àiren jiào Xiǎoqīng.

Page 29 Now you're talking!

1 ● **Nà shì nǐ zhàngfu ma?**
   ◆ Shìde, nà shì wǒ(de) zhàngfu.
   ● **Zhè shì nǐ nǚ'ér ma?**
   ◆ Shìde, zhè shì wǒ(de) nǚ'ér.
   ● **Tā jǐ suì le?**
   ◆ Tā shíyī suì.
   The daughter is 11.

2 ● Nǐ jiào shénme?
   ◆ **Wǒ jiào Steve.**

- Nǐ cóng nǎr lái?
- **Wǒ cóng Exeter lái.**
- Nǐ jiéhūn le ma?
- **Wǒ jiéhūn le.**
- Nǐ tàitai jiào shénme?
- **Tā jiào Olga.**
- Nǐmen yǒu háizi ma?
- **Wǒmen yǒu liǎng ge háizi.**
- Nǐ érzi jǐ suì le?
- **Tā bā suì.**
- Nǐ nǚ'ér ne?
- **Tā liù suì.**

Page 30 Quiz

1 a younger brother; *2* 44; *3* 79 qīshíjiǔ; *4* ge; *5* liǎng, háizi; *6* nǐ duō dà le?; *7* nǚ'ér, tàitai, māma, wàipó; *8* Zhè shì Zhōng Wěi zhǔrèn.

Unit 4

Pages 32-33 Ordering tea, coffee and other drinks

2 • Nǐmen yào shénme?
- **Yī** bēi chá.
- Wǒ yào sān **bēi** kāfēi.
- **Wǒmen yào** liǎng bēi **chá.**
- Gěi nǐmen.
- Xièxie.
- **Bú xiè.**
They order two cups of tea.

3 • Xiānsheng, nǐ yào hē shénme?
- **Wǒ yào yī bēi hóng chá**, xièxie.
- Xiǎojie, nǐ yào hē shénme?
- **Wǒ yào yī bēi lǜ chá**, xièxie.
- Bú kèqi.
Lín Guóqiáng: black tea; Zhào Měili: green tea.

5 • Nín yào shénme?
- Wǒ yào yī guàn kělè hé liǎng guàn píjiǔ.
He wants a cola and two beers.

6 • Wǒ yào sì píng píjiǔ.
- Sì píng píjiǔ, xièxie.
- Nín yào shénme?
- Wǒ yào yī bēi júzi zhī.
- Yī bēi júzi zhī, xièxie.

- Nǐmen yào hē shénme?
- Sān píng kuàngquán shuǐ.
- Sān píng kuàngquán shuǐ, xièxie.
- Yī bēi pútáojiǔ hé liǎng guàn kělè.
- Yī bēi pútáojiǔ hé liǎng guàn kělè, xièxie.
4 bottles of beer; 1 glass of orange juice; 3 bottles of mineral water; 1 glass of wine and 2 cans of cola.

7 liǎng bēi chá; yī bēi shuǐ; yī píng kuàngquán shuǐ; wǔ guàn kělè; liù píng píjiǔ; yī píng pútáojiǔ; sì bēi júzi zhī.

Page 34 Offering someone a drink

2 • Nǐ hǎo Zhāng Méi, nǐ hǎo Riley xiānsheng. Qǐng jìn, qǐng jìn.
- Lǐ Wěi, nǐ hǎo ma?
- Wǒ hěn hǎo. Qǐng zuò. Zhāng Méi, nǐ hē shénme?
- Wǒ hē lǜ chá, xièxie.
- Riley xiānsheng, nín yào hē shénme?
- Wǒ hē hóng chá. Xièxie.
- Nín yào jiā niúnǎi ma? Nín yào jiā táng ma?
- Bú yào, xièxie.
- Bú xiè.
Zhāng Méi: green tea; Jon Riley: black tea. No milk or sugar.

3 • Nǐ hǎo, Zhāng Méi, qǐng jìn.
- Xièxie, Lín xiānsheng, nín hǎo ma?
- Wǒ hěn hǎo. Qǐng zuò. Nǐ hē chá ma?
- Wǒ yào hóng chá.
- Qǐng hē chá.
- Zhè ge chá hěn hǎohē.
- Xièxie.

Page 35 Making choices

2 • Riley xiānsheng, Braun tàitai, nǐmen hǎo. Qǐng jìn, qǐng zuò.
- Xièxie, Lǐ Wéi Zhǔrèn, nǐ hǎo ma?
- Wǒ hěn hǎo. Nǐmen yào hē shénme? Riley xiānsheng, nǐ hē chá háishi kāfēi?
- Wǒ hē lǜ chá, xièxie.

- Braun tàitai, nǐ ne? Chá háishi kāfēi?
- ◆ Wǒ yào kāfēi jiā niúnǎi. Bú yào táng, xièxie.
- Hollmann xiānsheng, nǐ ne?
- ◆ Wǒ yě yīyàng, xièxie.

Offered tea or coffee. Jon: green tea; Elke and Eric: coffee with milk, no sugar.

3 ● Jon, Lisa, wǒ qǐng nǐmen hē jiǔ. Nǐmen yào hē shénme?
- ◆ Wǒ hē pútáojiǔ.
- ● Wǒ yě yīyàng.
- ◆ Bái pútáojiǔ háishi hóng pútáojiǔ?
- ● Wǒ yào hóng pútáojiǔ xièxie.
- ◆ Lisa, nǐ yào bái pútáojiǔ háishi hóng pútáojiǔ?
- ● Wǒ yào bái pútáojiǔ, xièxie.
- ◆ Wǒ yào píjiǔ. … Xiānsheng, wǒmen yào yī bēi hóng pútáojiǔ, yī bēi bái pútáojiǔ hé yī bēi píjiǔ.
- ● … Gān bēi, gān bēi.

Zhāng Méi: beer, Jon: red wine and Lisa: white wine.

4 *a* Nǐ yào lǜ chá háishi huā chá; *b* hóng pútáojiǔ háishi bái pútáojiǔ; *c* kuàngquán shuǐ háishi júzi zhī; *d* píjiǔ háishi kělè?

Page 36 Put it all together

1 *a* Bú kèqi; *b* Wǒ yào yì bēi lǜ chá; *c* Xièxie; *d* Wǒmen dōu hē chá; *e* Bú yào, xièxie.

2 *a* 3 glasses of red wine and 1 bottle of cola; *b* 2 cups of black tea, 5 cups of coffee and 1 cup of iced black tea; *c* 9 cans of orange juice, 4 bottles of mineral water; *d* 1 bottle of beer, 1 glass of white wine, 2 cans of cola.

3 *a* **yī bēi** hóng pútáojiǔ; *b* **liù guàn** píjiǔ; *c* **liǎng píng** júzi zhī; *d* **qī bēi** nǎi chá; *e* **sì bēi** kāfēi; *f* **sān píng** píjiǔ; *g* **wǔ bēi** bái pútáojiǔ; *h* **yī píng** kuàngquán shuǐ.

4 Nín yào hē shénme? Zhè ge chá hěn hǎohē.

Nǐmen yào kuàngquán shuǐ háishi júzi zhī?/Nǐmen yào júzi zhī háishi kuàngquán shuǐ?
Wǒ yào yī píng kělè.

Page 37 Now you're talking

1 ● Nǐmen hǎo. Nǐmen yào shénme?
- ◆ **Wǒmen dōu yào chá.**
- ● Nǐmen yào shénme chá? Hóng chá, lǜ chá háishi huā chá?
- ◆ **Wǒ yào yī bēi lǜ chá.**
- ● Tāmen yào shénme chá?
- ◆ **Tāmen yào yī bēi hóng chá hé yī bēi huā chá.**
- ● Hǎo de. Gěi nǐmen chá.

2 ● Nín hǎo. Qǐng jìn, qǐng zuò.
- ◆ **Xièxie.**
- ● Bú xiè. Nín hē chá háishi kāfēi?
- ◆ **Wǒ hē chá xièxie.**
- ● Nín yào lǜ chá háishi hóng chá?
- ◆ **Wǒ yào hóng chá.**
- ● Nín yào jiā niúnǎi ma? Nín yào jiā táng ma?
- ◆ **Bú yào, xièxie.**
- ● Gěi nín.
- ◆ **Zhè ge chá hěn hǎohē.**

3 ● **Nǐ yào píjiǔ ma? Wǒ qǐng nǐ.**
- ◆ Wǒ hē hóng pútáojiǔ.
- ● **Yī bēi hóng pútáojiǔ hé yī píng píjiǔ.**
- ◆ Gěi nǐ yī bēi hóng pútáojiǔ hé yī píng píjiǔ.
- ● **Gān bēi!**

Page 38 Quiz

1 xièxie; *2* bú xiè/bú kèqi; *3* hóng; *4* sit down; *5* píng; *6* ge; *7* háishi; *8* Bú yào niúnǎi xièxie.

Checkpoint 1
Pages 39-42

1 *a* zǎoshang hǎo; *b* hěn gāoxìng rènshi nǐ; *c* zhè ge chá hěn hǎohē; *d* wǒ hěn hǎo, xièxie; *e* qǐng zuò; *f* wǒ bú yào, xièxie; *g* bú kèqi; *h* nǐ duō dà le?; *i* wǎn'ān; *j* zhè shì wǒde míngpiàn.

2 *a* jiǔbā; *b* guó; *c* Yīngwén;
d Àodàlìyà; *e* shuǐ; *f* wàipó;
g péngyou; *h* líng.

3 *a* Nǐ jiào shénme? *b* Nǐ duō dà le?
c Nǐ shì nǎ guó rén? *d* Nǐ zuò shénme
gōngzuò?

4 *a* ✗ èrshí-wǔ; *b* ✗ sìshí-qī; *c* ✓;
d ✗ jiǔshí-sì.

5 Hong Kong 00852; Japan 0081;
Indonesia 0062; Thailand 0066;
Singapore 0065; Vietnam 0084;
Malaysia 0060; Philippines 0063.

7 ● Nǐ shì nǎ guó rén?
 ◆ Wǒ shì **Yīngguórén**. Wǒ māma shì
 Zhōngguórén.
 ● Wǒ shì Běijīngrén. Nǐ lái Zhōngguó
 dùjià háishi gōngzuò?
 ◆ **Dùjià**.
 ● Nǐ jiào shénme?
 ◆ Nicola. Nǐ ne?
 ● Wǒ jiào Chén Guóqiáng.
 ◆ Nǐ duō dà le?
 ● Wǒ èrshísān suì. Nǐ ne?
 ◆ **Èrshíyī** suì. Wǒ shì **xuésheng**. Nǐ
 zuò shénme gōngzuò?
 ● Wǒ shì gōngchéngshī.
 ◆ Wǒ bàba yě shì **gōngchéngshī**
 ● Nicola, wǒ qǐng nǐ hē píjiǔ.
 ◆ Wǒ yào yī bēi júzi zhī, xièxie.
 Glass of orange juice.

8 *a* 13 shísān; *b* 15 shíwǔ; *c* 22 èrshí'èr;
d 30 sānshí.

9 *a* wǒ shì Zhōngguórén; *b* tā shì
Měiguórén.

10 *a* chá *tea*; *b* shuǐ *water*; *c* bái *white*;
d hóng *red*.

Unit 5

Pages 44-45 Asking what there is in town and whereabouts it is

3 Zhèr yǒu gōngyuán hé huāyuán. Yǒu
hěn duō shāngdiàn hé cānguǎn.
*Park, garden, many shops and
restaurants.*

4 ● Qǐng wèn, yǒu wǎngbā ma?
 ◆ Méi yǒu. Zhèr méi yǒu wǎngbā.
 ● Yǒu xīcānguǎn ma?
 ◆ Yǒu, yǒu hěn duō cānguǎn.
 ● Qǐng wèn, zhèr yǒu bówùguǎn ma?
 ◆ Yǒu.
 ● Yǒu fúzhuāng shìchǎng ma?
 ◆ Yǒu fúzhuāng shìchǎng.
 *internet café ✗; western restaurant ✓;
 museum ✓; clothes market ✓*

6 ● Shāngdiàn zài shì zhōngxīn;
 bówùguǎn zài shì zhōngxīn de běi
 biān. Zhèr yǒu gōngyuán. Cānguǎn
 zài gōngyuán pángbiān.
 ◆ Qǐng wèn, yǒu yínháng ma?
 ● Yǒu. Yínháng zài huāyuán duìmiàn.
 ◆ Yǒu wǎngbā ma?
 ● Méi yǒu wǎngbā.
 ◆ Xièxie.
 A restaurants; B bank; C museum.

7 ● Qǐng wèn, yǒu fúzhuāng shìchǎng
 ma?
 ◆ Fúzhuāng shìchǎng zài huǒchēzhàn
 de duìmiàn.
 Opposite the station.

Pages 46-47 Finding out how far places are and when they're open

2 ● Qǐng wèn, fùjìn yǒu méi yǒu
 yínháng?
 ◆ Yǒu, shì zhōngxīn yǒu yínháng.
 ● Yuǎn ma?
 ◆ Bù yuǎn, zǒulù wǔ fēnzhōng.
 In town centre, five minutes' walk.

3 ● Qǐng wèn, fùjìn yǒu méi yǒu chāojí
 shìchǎng?
 ◆ Fùjìn méi yǒu. Chāojí shìchǎng bú
 jìn, sān gōnglǐ yuǎn.
 ● Xièxie.
 3km away.

4 ● Qǐng wèn, yǒu yóuyǒngchí ma?
 ◆ Yǒu.
 ● Yuǎn ma?
 ◆ Bú jìn, hěn yuǎn. Yóuyǒngchí zài
 shì zhōngxīn de xī biān. Zǒulù
 sìshíwǔ fēnzhōng.

Not near, very far, 45 minutes' walk.

6 ● Yóuyǒngchí **měi tiān** kāimén
  ◆ Táocí bówùguǎn **xīngqītiān**, **xīngqīyī** hé **xīngqīsì** guānmén.
  ● **Xīngqīsān** yǒu zhǎnlǎnhuì.
  Swimming pool open every day; porcelain museum closed Sunday, Monday, Thursday; exhibition on Wednesday.

7 ● Yóujú jīntiān zǎoshang kāimén ma?
  ◆ Yóujú měi tiān kāimén.
  ● Xīngqīliù kāimén ma?
  ◆ Yóujú xīngqīliù shàngwǔ hé xiàwǔ kāimén. Xīngqīliù wǎnshang guānmén.
  ● Xīngqītiān kāimén ma?
  ◆ Xīngqītiān zǎoshang hé wǎnshang guānmén.

  1 xīngqīliù xiàwǔ; xīngqīliù shàngwǔ kāimén.

  2 xīngqīliù wǎnshang; xīngqītiān zǎoshang ; xīngqītiān wǎnshang guānmén.

Page 48 Put it all together

1 *a* the park isn't far; *b* there's no internet café; *c* the museum is opposite the bank; *d* there's no supermarket nearby; *e* twenty-five minutes' walk; *f* there are lots of shops; *g* the bank is next to the market.

2 *a* Sunday; *b* Monday to Saturday 8am to 5pm; Sunday 9am to 4pm; *c* 2pm and 6:30pm; *d* no, open only Friday to Saturday.

Page 49 Now you're talking

1 ● **Qǐng wèn, yǒu gōngyuán ma?**
  ◆ Yǒu. Hěn jìn – wǔ bǎi mǐ.
  ● **Zhèr yǒu shāngdiàn ma?**
  ◆ Yǒu hěn duō shāngdiàn; zài shì zhōngxīn.
  ● **Xièxie. Zàijiàn.**

2 ● **Fùjìn yǒu méi yǒu wǎngbā?**
  ◆ Méi yǒu. Wǎngbā zài shì zhōngxīn de běi biān. Yuǎn, hěn yuǎn, wǔ gōnglǐ.
  ● **Yóujú lí zhèr yuǎn ma?**
  ◆ Yóujú bù yuǎn. Zài shì zhōngxīn, zài yínháng pángbiān.
  ● **Yóujú bù yuǎn. Zài shì zhōngxīn, zài yínháng pángbiān. Xièxie.**
  ◆ Bú kèqi.
  ● **Yínháng jīntiān kāimén ma?**
  ◆ Jīntiān yínháng guānmén.
  ● **Míngtiān kāimén ma?**
  ◆ Shìde. Míngtiān kāimén.

Page 50 Quiz

1 qǐng wèn; *2* yóuyǒngchí *swimming pool*; *3* xiàwǔ; *4* next to; *5* Yǒu méi yǒu xǐcānguǎn? *6* méi yǒu, guānmén, jìn; *7* Yes, banks open every day in China; *8* hěnduō.

Unit 6
Pages 52-53 Asking the way and following directions

2 ● Qǐng wèn, zuìjìn de cèsuǒ zài nǎr?
  ◆ Cèsuǒ zài **lóushàng**, zài **sān céng**.
  ● Xièxie.
  Toilets upstairs, 2nd floor (UK).

3 ● Qǐng wèn, cèsuǒ zài nǎr?
  ◆ Duìbuqǐ, **wǒ bù zhīdao**.
  ● Zuìjìn de cèsuǒ zài **lóuxià**, zài **sān céng**.
  ◆ Duìbuqǐ, wǒ bù dǒng. Cèsuǒ zài lóuxià ma?
  ● Lóuxià.
  a wǒ bù zhīdao – she doesn't know; b downstairs, 2nd floor (UK).

4 ● Qǐng wèn, cèsuǒ **zài nǎr?**
  ◆ Cèsuǒ zài nǐde **zuǒ** biān. Jiù **zài** nàbiān.
  On the left.

6 ● Qǐng wèn, qù huǒchēzhàn zěnme zǒu?

- **Yìzhí zǒu, dào lùkǒu, wǎng zuǒ guǎi.**
Straight on as far as the crossroads, turn left.

7 ● Qǐng wèn, qù Xuéyuàn Lù zěnme zǒu?
- Xuéyuàn Lù … wǎng **běi** zǒu dào **hónglǜdēng**. Wǎng **yòu** guǎi, Xuéyuàn Lù zài nǐde **zuǒ** biān.

8 ● Duìbuqǐ, wǒ mí lù le. Qǐng wèn, qù Xuéyuàn Lù zěnme zǒu?
- Xuéyuàn Lù bù yuǎn. Wǎng běi zǒu. Zǒu dào dì yī ge lùkǒu, wǎng yòu guǎi. Yìzhí zǒu dào dì èr ge hónglǜdēng. Xuéyuàn Lù zài nǐde zuǒ biān.
● Wǒ wǎng běi zǒu dào lùkǒu, wǎng yòu guǎi, yìzhí zǒu dào dì èr ge hónglǜdēng. Xuéyuàn Lù zài wǒde zuǒ biān.
- Duì. Xuéyuàn Lù zài nǐde zuǒ biān.
● Xièxie.
A = Xueyuan Road.

Pages 54-55 Talking about where people live and getting hep to understand

2 ● George, nǐ zhù zài nǎr?
- Wǒ zhù zài jiāoqū.
● Nǐ ne, Jacquie? Nǐ zhù zài nǎr?
- Wǒ zhù zài nóngcūn.
● Fran, nǐ zhù zài nǎr?
- Wǒ yě zhù zài nóngcūn.
● Thomas, Lizzie, nǐmen zhù zài nǎr? Nǐmen zhù zài shì zhōngxīn ma?
- Wǒmen zhù zài hǎi biān.
George: suburbs; Jacquie: country; Fran: country; Thomas & Lizzie: by the sea.

3 ● Fēng Yīmín, nǐ ne? Nǐ zhù zài nǎr?
- Wǒ zhù zài Shànghǎi, zài hǎi biān. Wǒ jiějie yě zhù zài Shànghǎi, dànshì wǒ bàba hé māma zhù zài jiāoqū.
● Nǐde yéye hé nǎinai zhù zài Shànghǎi ma?

- Tāmen bú zhù zài Shànghǎi shì. Tāmen zhù zài nóngcūn, zài Shànghǎi běi biān
Fēng Yīmín: Shanghai, by the sea. Her sister: Shanghai. Her parents: in the suburbs. Her grandparents: in the country, north of Shanghai.

5 ● Zhè shì wǒ péngyou Měilì.
- Hěn gāoxìng rènshi nǐmen. Wǒ yě shì Shànghǎirén.
● Qǐng zài shuō yībiàn.
- Wǒ shì Shànghǎirén – wǒ cóng Shànghǎi lái. Wǒ zhù zài gōngyù, hǎi biān. Wǒde gōngyù zài èrshísān céng.
● Měilì, qǐng shuō màn yìdiǎn.
- Wǒde gōngyù zài èrshísān céng.
a in Shanghai, by the sea; b 22nd floor (UK).

6 ● Wǒ shēng zài Sūzhōu, xiànzài zhù zài Shànghǎi.
- Qǐng zài shuō yíbiàn.
● Wǒ zhù zài Shànghǎi, dànshì wǒ shēng zài Sūzhōu.
- Duìbuqǐ, Měilì, wǒ bù dǒng. Nǐ huì shuō Yīngyǔ ma?
● Huì shuō yìdiǎn. I was born in Sūzhōu but now – xiànzài – I live in Shànghǎi.
- Nǐde Yīngyǔ hěn hǎo!
● Nǎli, nǎli.

Page 56 Put it all together

1 *a* Qǐng zài shuō yībiàn; *b* Nǐ zhù zài Déguó ma?; *c* Wǒ bù zhīdao; *d* Wǒ shuō yìdiǎn Zhōngwén; *e* Qǐng shuō màn yìdiǎn; *f* Nǐ shuō Déwén ma?; *g* Wǒ bù dǒng.
Wǎng dōng guǎi *Turn towards the east.*

2 *a* shuō; *b* zài; *c* zhù; *d* zǒu; *e* zhīdao; *f* huì.

3 c; h; g; e or f; a; f or e; d; b.

Page 57 Now you're talking

1 ● Duìbuqǐ, zuìjìn de cèsuǒ zài nǎr?
  ◆ Cèsuǒ zài lóushàng, wǔ céng.
  ● Qǐng zài shuō yībiàn.
  ◆ Cèsuǒ zài lóushàng, wǔ céng.
  ● Xièxie.
  She said the toilets are upstairs on the fourth floor (UK).

2 ● Qǐng wèn, nǐ huì shuō Yīngyǔ ma?
  ◆ Duìbuqǐ. Bú huì.
  ● Qǐng wèn, qù Zhōngshān Fàndiàn zěnme zǒu?
  ◆ Wǎng dōng zǒu, dào dì èr ge hónglǜdēng, wǎng yòu guǎi.
  ● Duìbuqǐ, wǒ bù dǒng.
  ◆ Wǎng dōng zǒu, dào dì èr ge hónglǜdēng, wǎng yòu guǎi, yìzhí zǒu, jiù shì Zhōngshān Fàndiàn.
  ● Yuǎn ma?
  ◆ Bù yuǎn, zǒulù shíwǔ fēnzhōng.

3 ● Nǐ zhù zài nǎr?
  ◆ Wǔ zhù zài Xiānggǎng.
  ● Nǐde bàba hé māma yě zhù zài Xiānggǎng ma?
  ◆ Bù, tāmen zhù zài Shànghǎi. Wǒmen quán jiā dōu zhù zài nàr.
  ● Duìbuqǐ, wǒ bù dǒng quán jiā
  ◆ Quán jiā – bàba hé māma, jiějie, yéye hé nǎinai, wàigōng, wàipó …
  ● Wǒ dǒng le.
  ◆ Nǐ Zhōngwén shuō de hěn hǎo!
  ● Nǎli, nǎli.

Page 58 Quiz

1 Eastern capital; *2* women's;
3 Where's the cashpoint?, Where's the nearest cashpoint?; *4* left; *5* nǎli nǎli; *6* yǒu; *7* 10th floor; *8* Wǒ zài Běijīng gōngzuò. Nǐ zài Xiānggǎng gōngzuò ma?

Unit 7

Page 60 Understanding prices in renminbi

1 yī yuán
  yī jiǎo
  yī fēn
  shí yuán
  shí yuán sān jiǎo
  shí yuán sān jiǎo sì fēn
  wǔshí yuán
  bāshíwǔ yuán qī jiǎo wǔ fēn

2 *a* bā yuán
  b bā jiǎo qī fēn
  c shíjiǔ yuán wǔ jiǎo
  d sìshí'èr yuán
  e liùshísì yuán wǔ jiǎo wǔ fēn
  f jiǔshí yuán jiǔ jiǎo jiǔ fēn

4 ● Bōluó duōshao qián?
  ◆ Sì yuán wǔ jiǎo.
  ● Xiāngjiāo duōshao qián?
  ◆ Sān yuán qián yī jīn.
  ● Mángguǒ duōshao qián?
  ◆ Liù yuán.
  ● Píngguǒ ne?
  ◆ Liǎng yuán qián yī jīn.
  ● Lìzhī duōshao qián?
  ◆ Shí yuán wǔ jiǎo qián yī jīn.
  ● Wǒ mǎi yī jīn.
  pineapple ¥4.50, bananas ¥3, mango ¥6, apples ¥2, lychees ¥10.50.

Page 61 Asking for what you want

3 ● Nín hǎo. Nín mǎi shénme?
  ◆ Wǒ yào mǎi míngxìnpiàn
  ● Yào duōshao?
  ◆ Wǒ mǎi zhè ge, nà ge, wǔ ge zhè ge. Duōshao qián?
  ● Shísì yuán.
  Postcards, cost ¥14 for 7 (this one, that one, 5 of those).

4 ● Hái yào biéde ma?
  ◆ **Wǒ mǎi zhè ge màozi.** Duōshao qián?
  ● Shí yuán.
  ◆ **Wǒ yào fángshàiyóu.**

- Fángshàiyóu èrshísān yuán wǔ jiǎo.
- **Yǒu lǚyóu dìtú ma?**
- Duìbuqǐ, méi yǒu. Hái yào biéde ma?
- Bú yào le, xièxie. **Qiǎokèlì duōshao qián?**
- Liù yuán.
- Wǒ mǎi yī bāo qiǎokèlì. Yīgòng duōshao qián?
- **Yīgòng, wǔshísān yuán wǔ jiǎo.**
- Xièxie.
- Zàijiàn.

She spent ¥53.50 altogether.

Page 62 Shopping in a department store

2
- Nín xiǎng mǎi shénme?
- Wǒ zài zhǎo lǐngdài.
- Hǎo de. Zhè shì zhēnsī lǐngdài.
- Yǒu qítā yánsè ma?
- Wǒmen yǒu lánsè, hóngsè, lǜsè, huángsè.
- Wó mǎi lánsè de lǐngdài.
  Wǒ zài zhǎo yángróng pījiān wéijīn.
- Hǎo de. Wǒmen yǒu hēisè, hóngsè, báisè, lánsè, huángsè, lǜsè.
- Hēisè. Wó mǎi hēisè pījiān. Duōshao qián?
- Yī bǎi sānshí'èr yuán.

Blue tie; black pashmina.

3
- Nín xiǎng mǎi shénme?
- Wǒ zài zhǎo chènshān. Báisè chènshān. Wǒ xiǎng kànkan nà jiàn.
- Nín yào duō dà de?
- Zhōng hào. Wǒ kěyǐ shìshi ma?
- Kěyǐ.
- Tài xiǎo le. Yǒu dà hào ma?

a false, he wants a white shirt; b true; c true.

Page 63 Bargaining

2
- Zhè ge Zhōngwén jiào shénme?
- Shānshuǐ huà.
- Zhè ge **hěn piàoliang**. Duōshao qián?
- Yī qiān yuán.

- Yǒu xiǎo de ma?
- Duìbuqǐ, méi yǒu.
- **Piányi yìdiǎn ba?**
- Zhè ge **hěn piàoliang**. Jiǔ bǎi wǔ shí yuán.
- **Tài guì le**. Jiǔ bǎi **yuán, zěnmeyàng?**
- **Hǎo ba**.

Final price ¥900.

3
- Nǐ hǎo. Nǐ mǎi shénme?
- Nà ge zhēnzhū ěrhuán duōshao qián?
- Sān bǎi bāshí yuán.
- Tài guì le! Xiǎo zhēnzhū. Piányi yìdiǎn ba?
- Hěn piàoliang de zhēnzhū. Bú guì.
- Tài guì le. Yī bǎi yuán?
- Èr bǎi wǔshí yuán.
- Yī bǎi wǔshí yuán.
- Èr bǎi yuán, zěnmeyàng?
- Hǎo ba. Èr bǎi yuán.

a ¥380; b ¥200.

Page 64 Put it all together

1 ¥21.77: èrshíyī yuán qī jiǎo qī fēn

2 a **guì** *expensive*, the rest are colours;
b **qiǎokèlì** *chocolate*, the rest are fruit; c **zhēnsī** *silk*, the rest are shops;
d **piàoliang** *beautiful*, the rest are sizes; e **míngxìnpiàn** *postcards*, the rest are clothing.

3 a Nín xiǎng **mǎi** shénme?
b Wǒ zài **zhǎo** chènshān.
c **Zhè** shì zhēnsī chènshān.
d **Yǒu** qítā yánsè **ma**?
e **Wǒmen** yǒu báisè, lánsè, huángsè, **lǜsè** …
f Wǒ mǎi lánsè de chènshān. Wǒ kěyǐ **shìshi** ma?

4
- Nín mǎi shénme?
- Wǒ yào mǎi fēngzheng.
- Zhè ge hěn piàoliang.
- Duōshao qián?
- Èr bǎi wǔshí yuán.
- Tài guì le! Piányi yìdiǎn ba?
- Èr bǎi yuán, zěnmeyàng?

◆ Hǎo ba.
a kite; 200 yuan.

Page 65 Now you're talking

1 ● Nǐ hǎo. Nǐ mǎi shénme?
◆ **Xiāngjiāo duōshao qián?**
● Sān kuài yī jīn.
◆ **Wǒ mǎi yī jīn xiāngjiāo**
● Hái yào biéde ma?
◆ **Wǒ mǎi liǎng ge nà ge.**
● Qiǎokèlì duōshao qián?
◆ Bā yuán wǔ jiǎo.
● **Qǐng zài shuō yíbiàn.**
◆ Bā yuán wǔ jiǎo.

2 ● Nín mǎi shénme?
◆ **Wǒ zài zhǎo zhēnsī lǐngdài.**
Wǒ xiǎng kànkan zhè ge.
● Hěn piàoliang de lǐngdài.
◆ **Yǒu qítā yánsè ma?**
● Wǒmen yǒu lánsè, hóngsè, lǜsè, huángsè.

3 ● Hěn piàoliang de xiàngliàn. Dà zhēnzhū … liǎng qiān liù bǎi yuán.
◆ **That is 2,600 yuan.**
Tài guì le.
● Bú guì!
◆ **Piányi yìdiǎn ba?**
Yī qiān liǎng bǎi yuán zěnmeyàng?
● Hǎo ba.
◆ **Xièxie. Zàijiàn.**

Page 66 Quiz

1 10, 2; *2* Do you want anything else?; *3* zhù *live*, shuō *speak*; *4* wǔ ge nà ge; *5* XXL; *6* bú shì, bú yào, méi yǒu; *7* Wǒ zài zhǎo chúnmáo shàngyī; *8* Tài hòu le.

Checkpoint 2
Pages 67–70

1 ● Qǐng wèn, fùjìn yǒu méi yǒu **yínháng**?
◆ Yǒu. Yìzhí zǒu dào dì yī ge hónglǜdēng, wǎng zuǒ guǎi …
● Duìbuqǐ, qǐng shuō màn yìdiǎn. Wǒ bù dǒng.

◆ Yìzhí zǒu dào hónglǜdēng, wǎng zuǒ guǎi. Yínháng zài Shànghǎi Lù, zài nǐde yòu biān.

● Qǐng wèn, **huǒchēzhàn** zài nǎr?
◆ Duìbuqǐ, wǒ bù zhīdao. Wǒ bú shì běndìrén.
● Qǐng wèn, huǒchēzhàn zài nǎr?
◆ Zǒu dào hónglǜdēng, wǎng yòu guǎi. Yìzhí zǒu, dào lùkǒu, wǎng zuǒ guǎi dào Xuéyuàn Lù. Yìzhí zǒu, huǒchēzhàn jiù zài nàbiān.
● Yuǎn ma?
◆ Bù yuǎn, hěn jìn, wǔ bǎi mǐ. Zǒulù wǔ fēnzhōng.
● Qǐng wèn, fùjìn yǒu **chāojí shìchǎng** ma?
◆ Chāojí shìchǎng zài shì zhōngxīn. Yìzhí zǒu dào hónglǜdēng, wǎng zǒu guǎi. Wǎng yòu guǎi dào Dōng Fāng Lù. Nàr yǒu yī jiā chāojí shìchǎng, zài nǐde yòu biān. Zài yóujú pángbiān.

a yínháng bank E, b huǒchēzhàn station A; c chāojí shìchǎng supermarket C.

2 *a* false: Yǒu liǎng jiā jiǔbā; *b* true; *c* false: Bówùguǎn zài yínháng duìmiàn.

3 yī bēi kǎbùqínuò: shíwǔ yuán ¥15
liǎng ge hànbǎo bāo: sānshí yuán ¥30
yī ge bǐsà bǐng: shísì yuán, wǔ jiǎ ¥14.50
yī píng xiāngbīn: jiǔshíqī yuán ¥97
yī píng báilándì: bāshíqī yuán ¥87
sān bēi wēishìjì liùshíjiǔ yuán ¥69

4 xīngqīyī; xīngqī'èr; xīngqīsān; xīngqīsì; xīngqīwǔ; xīngqīliù; xīngqītiān

5 *a* 14; *b* 90; *c* 55; *d* 73; *e* 62; *f* 十; *g* 二十二; *h* 八十; *i* 十六

6 *a* zhǎlǎnhuì; *b* fàndiàn; *c* bǎihuò shāngdiàn; *d* jiǔbā; *e* shuǐguǒdiàn.

7 *a* Kěyǐ shìshi ma?; *b* Nǐ huì shuō Yīngyǔ ma?; *c* Yǒu dà hào ma?; *d* Tài guì le, piányi yìdiǎn ba; *e* Wǒ xiǎng kànkan zhè ge; *f* Qǐng

shuō màn yìdiǎn; g Qǐng zài shuō yībiàn; h Duìbuqǐ.

8 dōng, nán, běi
dà, xiǎo, guì
shìchǎng, chāojí shìchǎng, shāngdiàn
chènshān, màozi, lǐngdài
xīcānguǎn, jiǔbā, cānguǎn
nóngcūn, hǎi biān, jiāoqū
xiāngjiāo, píngguǒ, lìzhī

9 a yēzi coconut; b yīngtáo cherry; c xī guā watermelon; d níngméng lemon.

10 a shop; b book; c flower; d bread; e shoe; f stationery.

Unit 8

Pages 72-73 Finding a hotel room and saying how long you want to stay

2 ● Nǐ hǎo. Yǒu kòng fángjiān ma?
   ◆ Dānrén fángjiān háishi shuāngrén fángjiān?
   ● Shuāngrén fángjiān dài yùshì.
   ◆ Huānyíng guānglín.
   ● Wǎnshang hǎo. Yǒu fángjiān ma?
   ◆ Yǒu.
   ● Wǒ yào dānrén jiān dài yùshì hé kōngtiáo.
   ◆ Nǐ hǎo. Wǒ yào shuāngrén jiān dài kōngtiáo.
   ● Duìbuqǐ, méi yǒu kōngtiáo.
   ◆ Huānyíng guānglín. Wǎnshang hǎo.
   ● Wǒmen yào liǎngrén fángjiān dài yùshì hé kōngtiáo.
   ◆ Hǎo ba.
   1 double room with en suite;
   2 single room with en suite and air conditioning; 3 double room with air conditioning; 4 twin room with en suite and air conditioning.

3 ● Bāo zǎocān ma?
   ◆ Bāo. Cānguǎn zài sì céng.
   a Bāo, Bù bāo; b The restaurant's on the 3rd floor.

5 ● Nín zhù jǐ tiān?
   ◆ Wǒ zhù **yī ge xīngqī**.
   ● Nǐmen yào zhù jǐ tiān?
   ◆ **Cóng jīntiān dào xīngqīsān.**
   ● Nín zhù jǐ wǎn?
   ◆ Wǒ zhù **liǎng ge wǎnshang**.

6 ● Wèi, nǐ hǎo, shì Mín Háng Fàndiàn.
   ◆ Yǒu kòng fángjiān ma?
   ● Nǐ shénme shíhou zhù?
   ◆ **Shíyīyuè liù hào.**
   ● Wèi. Shì Mín Háng Fàndiàn.
   ◆ Nǐ hǎo. Wǒ yào shuāngrén fángjiān dài yùshì. **Liùyuè shísì hào xīngqīliù.**
   ● Qǐng shāo děng … Duìbuqǐ, wǒmen zhù mǎn le.
   ◆ Wèi.
   ● Yǒu kòng fángjiān ma?
   ◆ Nǐ shénme shíhou zhù?
   ● **Cóng jīntiān dào wǔyuè èrshíwǔ hào.**
   ◆ Qǐng shāo děng.
   a 6th November; b on Saturday, 14th June (not available); c from today until 25th May.

Page 74 Checking in

2 ● Nǐ hǎo. Wǒ yùdìng le fángjiān.
   ◆ Nín guì xìng?
   ● Wǒ xìng Qín. Wǒ yùdìng le shuāngrén fángjiān, zhù sì ge wǎnshang.
   ◆ Qǐng tián zhè zhāng biǎo …. Gěi nín yàoshi. Fángjiān hàomǎ shì liù qī líng.
   a Qín; b double room; c 4 nights; d fill in a form; e 670.

3 ● Wǒ yùdìng le yī ge wǎnshang shuāngrén jiān.
   ◆ Nín guì xìng?
   ● Wǒ xìng Lǐ, jiào Lǐ Ěr.
   ◆ Nín hǎo, Lǐ xiānsheng. Qǐng gěi wǒ nínde hùzhào.
   ● Gěi nǐ.
   ◆ Xièxie. Fángjiān hàomǎ shì yī èr bā jiǔ.

- Huānyíng guānglín. Nín yùdìng fángjiān le ma?
- Wǒ yùdìng le yī ge xīngqī dānrén jiān. Wǒ xìng Zhāng.
- Nín hǎo, Zhāng xiǎojie. Qǐng tián zhè zhāng biǎo.
- Wǒde fángjiān hàomǎ shì duōshao?
- Yī jiǔ líng sān. Zhè shì nínde yàoshi.
- Xièxie.
- Huānyíng guānglín. Nín guì xìng?
- Wǒ xìng Gāo. Wǒ yùdìng le sān ge wǎnshang shuāngrén jiān.
- Nín hǎo, Gāo tàitai. Zhè shì nínde yàoshi. Nínde fángjiān hàomǎ shì èr liù qī bā.
- Yǒu diàntī ma?
- Yǒu, zài zuǒbiān. Qǐng gēn wǒ lái.

Lǐ xiānsheng: double room for 1 night, room no. 1289; Zhāng xiǎojie: single room for 1 week, room no. 1903; Gāo tàitai: double room for 3 nights, room no, No.2678.

4 *The lifts are on the left.*

Page 75 Making requests

2
- Xiǎojie. Qǐng wèn, wǒ néng yòng xìnyòngkǎ fù ma?
- Néng.
- Nǐ néng bù néng liù diǎn jiào xǐng wǒ?
- Dāngrán kěyǐ.

He wants a) to pay by credit card, b) a wake-up call at 6.

3
- Xiǎojie, wǒ kěyǐ **bǎ wǒde xínglǐ liú zài zhèr** ma?
- Kěyǐ.
- Xiǎojie, nǐ néng bù néng **gěi wǒ jiào yī liàng chūzūchē**?
- Dāngrán kěyǐ.
- Wǒ néng **yòng hùliánwǎng jiēkǒu** ma?
- Duìbuqǐ …
- Wǒ néng **yòng zhè ge diànhuà** ma?
- Dāngrán kěyǐ.
- Xiǎojie, qǐng wèn. Duōshao qián?

- Èr bǎi wǔshí yuán.
- Wǒ néng **yòng xìnyòngkǎ fù** ma?
- Néng.

Page 76 Put it all together

1 a wǒ yào; b nǐ néng bù néng; c wǒmen zhù; d wǒ kěyǐ … ma; e gěi nǐ; f qǐng; g wǒmen néng … ma.

2 a Yǒu kòng **dānrén jiān** ma?; b Wǒ yào **shuāngrén jiān dài yùshì** ; c Wǒ néng **yòng jiànshēnfáng** ma?; d Nǐ néng bù néng gěi wǒ jiào yī liàng **chūzūchē**?; e Qǐng gěi wǒ **yàoshi**.

3 a shí'èryuè èrshíwǔ hào; b shí'èryuè sānshíyī hào; c yīyuè yī hào; d èryuè shísì hào.

Page 77 Now you're talking

1
- Huānyíng guānglín. Wǒ néng bāngzhù nǐ ma?
- **Yǒu kòng fángjiān ma?**
- Shuāngrén jiān háishi liǎngrén jiān?
- **Liǎngrén jiān, dài yùshì.**
- Nǐ yào zhù jǐ wǎn?
- **Zhǐ yào jīnwǎn.**
- Yǒu kòng fángjiān.
- **Fángjiān duōshao qián?**
- Liù bǎi yuán.
- **Bāo zǎocān ma?**
- Bāo zǎocān.

2
- **Wǒ yùdìng le fángjiān.**
- Nín guì xìng?
- **Wǒ xìng Marshall.**
- Dānrén jiān dài kōngtiáo. Sān ge wǎnshang.
- **Wǒ zhù yí ge xīngqī.**
- Qǐng shāo děng. Hǎo, yī ge xīngqī. Dào sānyuè liù hào. Qǐng gěi wǒ nínde hùzhào.
- **Gěi nǐ hùzhào. Wǒ kěyǐ yòng xìnyòngkǎ fù** ma?
- Dāngrán kěyǐ.

Page 78 Quiz

1 passport; 2 Měiguórén *American*; 3 Bāo zǎocān ma?; 4 qīyuè *July*, jiǔyuè *September*; 5 taxi; 6 Nǐ néng

bù néng qī diǎn jiào xǐng wǒ?; 7 Tā zhù liǎng ge xīngqī; 8 a Yǒu xǐyīfáng ma?, b Wǒ néng yòng xǐyīfáng ma?

Unit 9

Page 80 Saying where you're going

2 • Nǐ hǎo. Wǒ néng bāngzhù nǐ ma?
  ◆ Wǒ yào qù Tiān'ānmén.
  • Nǐ shénme shíhou qù?
  ◆ **Xiànzài**.
  • Nǐ kěyǐ zuò **gōnggòng qìchē** huòzhě **chūzūchē**.
  Bus, taxi; he wants to go now.

3 • Wǒ yào **qù** shì zhōngxīn.
  ◆ Nǐ **shénme shíhou** qù? Jīntiān **háishi** míngtiān?
  • Míngtiān.
  • Nǐ kěyǐ zuò dìtiě **huòzhě** chūzūchē.
  • Hǎo. Nǐ **yǒu** dìtú ma?
  • Gěi nǐ.
  • Xièxie.
  • Bú xiè.

Page 81 Asking about public transport

2 • Duìbuqǐ. Wǒ yào qù Chángchéng. Yǒu gōnggòng qìchē ma?
  ◆ Yǒu. Zuò jiǔ yāo bā lù chē.
  • Duō jiǔ néng dào?
  ◆ Yī ge xiǎoshí.
  • Duìbuqǐ. Zuò jǐ lù chē qù Běihǎi Gōngyuán?
  ◆ Sān èr liù.
  • Qǐng wèn, yǒu qù Tiān'ānmén de gōnggòng qìchē ma?
  ◆ Méi yǒu. Tiān'ānmén bù yuǎn, bù yuǎn.
  • Duō jiǔ néng dào?
  ◆ Zǒulù shí fēnzhōng.
  • Xièxie.
  ◆ Zhè ge chē qù Yōnghégōng ma?
  • Qù.
  ◆ Chē shénme shíhou kāi?
  • Shí fēnzhōng yǐhòu.
  ◆ Duìbuqǐ. Zhè lù chē qù Yíhéyuán ma?

• Bú qù, nín zuò sānshíwǔ lù chē. Wǔ fēnzhōng néng dào.
◆ Shénme shíhou yǒu chē qù Gùgōng?
• Měi shíwǔ fēnzhōng.
◆ Duō jiǔ néng dào?
• Wǔ fēnzhōng. Hěn jìn.
Beihai Park: bus no. 326; Forbidden City: bus every 15 minutes, takes 5 minutes; Lama Temple every 10 minutes; Tiananmen Square: no bus, 10 minutes' walk; The Great Wall: bus no. 918, takes 1 hour; Summer Palace: bus no. 35, takes 5 minutes to arrive.

Page 82-83 Finding out train times and buying tickets

2 • Duìbuqǐ, xià yī bān qù Chángzhōu de huǒchē jǐ diǎn kāi?
  ◆ Bā diǎn wǔshí.
  • Duìbuqǐ, xià yī bān qù Nánjīng de huǒchē jǐ diǎn kāi?
  ◆ Liǎng diǎn sānshí'èr.
  • Xià yī tàng qù Shànghǎi de huǒchē jǐ diǎn kāi?
  ◆ Wǎnshang jiǔ diǎn sānshíliù.
  • Wǒ yào qù Shěnyáng. Zǎoshang yǒu huǒchē ma?
  ◆ Yǒu. Liù diǎn sìshíjiǔ kāi.
  • Qù Qínhuángdǎo de huǒchē jǐ diǎn kāi?
  ◆ Shíyī diǎn èrshísān.
  Changzou 8.50; Nanjing 2.32; Shanghai 9.36pm; Shenyang 6.49am; Qinhuangdao 11.23.

3 • Duìbuqǐ, xià yī bān qù Xī'ān de huǒchē jǐ diǎn kāi?
  ◆ Shíwǔ fēnzhōng hòu. Qī diǎn líng sān.
  • Huǒchē jǐ diǎn dào Xī'ān ?
  ◆ Zǎoshang liù diǎn sìshísì fēn.
  3 a false – it leaves in 15 minutes; b true; c false – it arrives at 6.44pm.

5 ● Wǒmen qù Sūzhōu.
  ◆ Nǐmen yào mǎi jǐ zhāng?
  ● Sì zhāng piào.
  ◆ Dānchéng háishi wǎngfǎn?
  ● Wǎngfǎn.
  ◆ Nǐmen yào yìngzuò háishi ruǎnzuò?
  ● Ruǎnzuò duōshao qián?
  ◆ Ruǎnzuò èrshíbā yuán, yìngzuò shí yuàn.
  ● Wǒ mǎi sì zhāng ruǎnzuò piào. Lam xiǎojie mǎi **sì** zhāng **wǎngfǎn** piào. Tā yào ruǎnzuò piào.

6 ● Wǎnshang hǎo. Wǒ yào qù Běijīng. Xià yī tàng huǒchē jǐ diǎn kāi?
  ◆ Qī diǎn bàn. Z-shísān cì chē.
  ● Huǒchē jǐ diǎn dào Běijīng?
  ◆ Zǎoshang qī diǎn líng liù.
  ● Hǎo de. Yǒu piào ma?
  ◆ Yǒu. Jǐ zhāng piào?
  ● Yī zhāng piào.
  ◆ Dānchéng háishi wǎngfǎn?
  ● Dānchéng.
  ◆ Nín yào ruǎnzuò háishi ruǎnwò?
  ● Ruǎnzuò.
  ◆ Sān bǎi qīshí'èr yuán
  ● Wǒ kěyǐ yòng xìnyòngkǎ fù ma?
  ◆ Dāngrán kěyǐ.
  Destination: Beijing; Departure 7.30, arrival 7.06 am; single ticket; soft seat; 372 yuan.

Page 84 Put it all together

1 *a* 4; *b* 3; *c* 1; *d* 2; *e* 6; *f* 5.

2 *a* zǎoshang qī diǎn bàn; *b* wǎnshang liù diǎn èrshísān; *c* zhōngwǔ shí'èr diǎn yī kè; *d* shàngwǔ shí diǎn sìshí; *e* xiàwǔ sì diǎn líng wǔ; *f* zǎoshang wǔ diǎn chà yī kè.

3 *a* **zǎocān** *breakfast*, the rest are parts of the day; *b* **zìxíngchē** *bicycle*, the rest are trains; *c* **píngguǒ** *apple*, the rest relate to time; *d* **hùzhào** *passport*, the rest are train seating; *e* **piào** *ticket*, the rest relate to telling the time.

4 *a* **Yǒu qù Chángchéng de gōnggòng qìchē ma?** Is there a bus to the Great Wall?
  b **Nǐ shénme shíhou qù Běijīng?** When are you going to Beijing?
  c **Xià yī tàng qù Nánjīng de huǒchē jǐ diǎn kāi?** What time is the next train to Nanjing?

Page 85 Now you're talking

1 ● **Yǒu qù Yíhéyuán de gōnggòng qìchē ma?**
  ◆ Yǒu. Qīshíbā lù chē. Měi shí fēnzhōng yī tàng.
  Bus no. 78, every 10 minutes.

  ● **Duō jiǔ néng dào?**
  ◆ Èrshíwǔ fēnzhōng.
  ● **Piào duōshao qián?**
  ◆ Shíliù yuán.
  ● **Wǒ mǎi liǎng zhāng (piào).**
  ◆ Gěi nǐ.
  ● **Xièxie.**
  ◆ Bú xiè.

2 ● **Xià yī tàng qù Xī'ān de huǒchē jǐ diǎn kāi?**
  ◆ Liù diǎn sìshíwǔ fēn.
  ● **Huǒchē jǐ diǎn dào Xī'ān?**
  ◆ Zǎoshang qī diǎn líng wǔ.
  ● **Wǒ yào yī zhāng piào.**
  ◆ Dānchéng háishi wǎngfǎn?
  ● **Dānchéng.**
  ◆ Nǐ yào ruǎnzuò piào ma?
  ● **Wǒ yào ruǎnwò. Duōshao qián?**
  ◆ Liùshí'èr yuán. Gěi nǐ. Yí lù píng ān.

Page 86 Quiz

1 8.45, jiǔ diǎn sānshí (fēn), jiǔ diǎn bàn; *2* a bus; *3* to buy tickets; *4* háishi; *5* express, T; *6* ruǎnwò, standing; *7* every half hour/in half an hour's time; *8* Yínháng jǐ diǎn guānmén?.

Unit 10

Page 88 Choosing a place to eat

2 ● Wǒmen wǎnshang chī shénme?
  ◆ Wǒ xǐhuan chuāncài.
  ● Wǒ yě xǐhuan chuāncài.
  ◆ Wǒ bù xǐhuan chuāncài - hěn là.
    Wǒmen chī jiǎozi, hǎo bù hǎo?
  ● Wǒ bù xǐhuan jiǎozi. Wǒ gèng
    xǐhuan jiāngsūcài. Wǒmen chī
    jiāngsūcài, hǎo ma?
  ◆ Hǎo zhǔyi. Wǒ hěn xǐhuan
    jiāngsūcài.
  *They decide on jiāngsūcài (Jiangsu
  cuisine).*

3 ● Nǐmen hǎo. Nǐmen jǐ wèi?
  ◆ Liǎng wèi.
  ● Qǐng zuò.
  ◆ Nǐmen hǎo. Nǐmen jǐ wèi?
  ● Wǒmen liù wèi.
  ◆ Qǐng zuò.
  ● Xièxie.
  a two; b six.

4 ● Zhè shì càidān. Nǐmen xiǎng hē
    shénme?
  ◆ Wǒ hē chá.
  ● Wǒ yě yīyàng.
  ◆ Wǒ gèng xǐhuan píjiǔ.
  ● Dà píng háishi xiǎo píng?
  ◆ Dà píng, xièxie.
  ● Wǒ yào pútáojiǔ, bái pútáojiǔ.
  *Tea; tea; beer (large bottle); white
  wine.*

Page 89 Understanding what's on the menu

2 *Fish soup, hot & sour soup. Boiled
  rice, egg fried rice, stir fried noodles.
  Sweet & sour chicken; stir fried lamb,
  roast duck, beef curry, marinated
  tofu, sweet & sour spare ribs, seasonal
  vegetables, sautéed broccoli with
  mushrooms.*

Page 90 Ordering a meal

2 ● Nǐmen diǎn cài ma?
  ◆ Diǎn.
  ● Zhǔcài yào shénme?
  ◆ Zhǔcài wǒmen yào yī ge tángcù
    páigǔ, yī ge gālí jīròu, liǎng zhī
    Běijīng kǎoyā, yī ge shícài.
  ● Zhǔshí yào shénme?
  ◆ Wǒmen dōu yào bái mǐfàn.
  ● Wǒ gèng xǐhuan dàn chǎofàn.
  ◆ Wǒ yào chǎomiàn.
  ● Nàme, qǐng lái yī wǎn dàn chǎofàn,
    yī wǎn chǎomiàn, sì wǎn mǐfàn.
  *1 sweet & sour spare ribs, 1 chicken
  curry, 2 Beijing roast ducks, 1 seasonal
  vegetables; 1 bowl egg fried rice, 1
  bowl stir fried noodles, 4 bowls boiled
  rice.*

3 ● Wǒ bù chī ròu – wǒ chī sù. Zhè ge
    cài yǒu méi yǒu ròu?
  ◆ Yǒu. Nín chī dàn ma?
  ● Bù chī dàn. Lǔshuǐ dòufu là bú là?
  ◆ Bù là, bú là.
  ● Nàme, qǐng lái yī ge lǔshuǐ dòufu,
    xièxie.
  *Chīsù means vegetarian. She orders
  marinated tofu.*

4 ● Amanda, nǐ xǐhuan mǐjiǔ?
  ◆ Wǒ bú zhīdào.
  ● Fúwùyuán, qǐng lái yī píng **mǐjiǔ**,
    zài lái yī ge **chāzi**. Xièxie.
  ◆ Gěi nín. Mànmàn chī.
  ● Gān bēi.
  He asks for rice wine and a fork.

Page 91 Expressing appreciation

2 ● Gòu ma? Hái yào biéde ma?
  ● Gòu le, xièxie. Tíng Huà, gòu ma?
  ● **Gòu le, gòu le.** Hěn hǎochī.
  ◆ Jiàn Zhōng, nǐ chī bǎo le ma?
  ● **Wǒ chī bǎo le, xièxie.**
  ◆ Amanda, nǐ chī bǎo le ma?
  ● **Wǒ chī bǎo le**, fàncài hěn hǎochī.
    Tài hǎo le!

3 ● Fàncài zěnme yàng?
  ◆ **Fàncài hěn hǎochī**, xièxie.
  ● Kǎoyā **fēicháng hǎo, tài hǎo le**!
  ◆ Qǐng jiézhàng.

- Qǐng shāo děng … Gěi nín.
- Jīntiān wǒ qǐngkè.
- Xièxie.
- Zàijiàn!

Page 92 Put it all together

1 g; h; c; d; a; f; e; b.

2 *a* wǒ bù xǐhuan yú; *b* wǒ bù chī yú;
c wǒ gèng xǐhuan yú; *d* wǒ hěn
xǐhuan yú; *e* yú tài hǎo le; *f* zhè ge yú
là ma.

3 *a* seafood soup; *b* beef soup; *c* sweet
& sour pork; *d* stir fried vegetables
and tofu; *e* lamb curry; *f* deep fried
prawns; *g* tomato and egg soup;
h fried eggs.

4 *a* Wǒ xǐhuan yuècài; *b* Nǐ xǐhuan mǐjiǔ
ma?; *c* Wǒ gèng xǐhuan píjiǔ;
d Wǒmen dōu hěn xǐhuan Zhōngcān.

Page 93 Now you're talking

1 ● Huānyíng guānglín. Qǐng wèn, jǐ
wèi.
◆ **Liǎng wèi.**
● Qǐng zuò. Nǐmen yào hē shénme?
◆ **Wǒmen dōu hē chá, xièxie.**
● Zhè shì càidān.
◆ **Xièxie.**
● Nǐmen diǎncài ma?
◆ **Yī ge chǎo niúròu hé yī zhī kǎoyā.**
● Zhǔshí yào shénme?
◆ **Yī wǎn mǐfàn hé yī wǎn miàntiáo.**
● Nǐmen yào kuàizi háishi chāzi?
◆ **Kuàizi, xièxie.**
● Gěi nín – yī ge chǎo niúròu hé yī
zhī kǎoyā, mǐfàn, miàntiáo. Hái yào
biéde ma?
◆ **Qǐng lái liǎng píng píjiǔ.**
● Hǎo. Mànmàn chī.
◆ Fàncài zěnmeyàng?
● **Fàncài hěn hǎochī.**
◆ **Qǐng jiézhàng.**
● Qǐng shāo děng.

Page 94 Quiz

1 sì wèi; *2* No, it's braised lamb; *3*
Fúwùyuán!; *4* dòuyá, the others are
seafood; *5* western food; *6 a* What
would you like as a staple? *b* What is
there/have you got as a staple?; *7* Yú
xiāng niúròu là bú là?; *8* Gālì niúròu
yǒu méi yǒu guǒrén?

Checkpoint 3

Pages 95-98

1 *b* Duìbuqǐ, zuìjìn de jiǔbā zài nǎr?

2 Nín hǎo. Nín hē shénme?
Yī píng píjiǔ.
Xiǎo de háishi dà de?
Dà de, xièxie.
Duōshao qián?
Èrshísì yuán.
Change: qīshíliù yuán.

3 *a* Cèsuǒ zài nǎr?; *b* Fùjìn yǒu méi
yǒu wǎngbā?; *c* Yóujú jīntiān kāimén
ma?; *d* Qù Xin Gang Wan Fàndiàn
zěnme zǒu?

4 ● Qù Xin Gang Wan Fàndiàn zěnme
zǒu?
◆ Wǎng běi zǒu. Zǒu dào
hónglǜdēng, wǎng zuǒ guǎi, yìzhí
zǒu dào yī ge lùkǒu, wǎng yòu
guǎi. Fàndiàn zài nǐde yòu biān.

*Go north. Go to the traffic lights, turn
left, go straight on as far as the first
crossroads, turn right. The hotel's on
your right.*

5 *a* **Xīngqīsì** qù Dàlián de **huǒchē**
jǐ diǎn kāi?; *b* Huǒchē jǐ diǎn **dào**
Dàlián?; *c* Duō shǎo qián yī zhāng
wǎngfǎn piào?

6 *d* Wǒ yùdìng le yī ge xīngqī de dānrén
jiān dài yùshì.

7 ● Nǐ hǎo. Wǒ yùdìng le yī ge xīngqī
de dānrén jiān dài yùshì.
◆ Xiānsheng, huānyíng guānglín. Nín
guìxìng? Qǐng gěi wǒ nínde hùzhào
… Xièxie. Gěi nín yàoshi – nínde

fángjiān hàomǎ shì èr bā sì jiǔ.
Diàntī zài nínde zuǒ biān.

8 • Nín hǎo. Nín mǎi shénme?
 ◆ **Wǒ xiǎng mǎi shǒutíbāo.**
 • Zhè ge hěn piàoliang. Zhè shì zhēn
   pí.
 ◆ **Tài dà le. Wǒ kěyǐ kànkan nà ge
   ma?**
 • Gěi nín. Zhè ge yě hěn piàoliang.
   Bú dà.
 ◆ **Wǒ hěn xǐhuan. Duōshao qián?**
 • Yī qiān èr bǎi yuán.
 ◆ **Tài guì le. Bā bǎi zěnmeyàng?**
 • Hǎo ba.
 ◆ **Wǒ kěyǐ yòng xìnyòngkǎ fù ma?**
 • Duìbuqǐ, bù kěyǐ.

9 *a* Wǒ jiào Tanaka Keiko; *b* Bú shì, wǒ
   shì Rìběnrén.

10 *a* Nǐ zhù zài nǎr? *b* Nǐ zuò shénme
   gōngzuò? *c* Nǐ jiéhūn le ma? *d* Nǐ
   yǒu háizi ma? *e* Tā jǐ suì le? *f* Nǐ
   huì shuō Yīngwén ma? *g* Nǐ xǐhuan
   Běijīng cài ma?

   Nǐ xìng shénme?; Nǐ jiào shénme?;
   Nǐ shì Měiguórén ma?; Nǐ zhù zài
   nǎr?; Nǐ zuò shénme gōngzuò?; Nǐ
   duō dà le?; Nǐ jiéhūn le ma?; Nǐ yǒu
   háizi ma?; Nǐ shuō Fǎwén ma?; Nǐ
   xǐhuan chuāncài ma?; Nǐde diànhuà
   hàomǎ shì shénme?

11 Míngtiān hé xīngqī'èr wǒ zài Běijīng
   gōngzuò. Xīngqī'èr wǎnshang wǒ
   qù Dàlián, wǒ zài Dàlián gōngzuò
   zhídào xīngqīsì xiàwǔ. Xīngqīsì
   wǎnshang hé xīngqīwǔ wǒ zāi
   Jǐnzhōu. Xīngqīliù wǒ qù Rìběn
   Dōngjīng … wǒde jiā!

12 *a* yú xiāng niúròu; *b* yóumèn dàxiā;
   c dòufu shāo yú; *d* Běijīng kǎoyā;
   e qīngzhēng quánjī.

   f **niúròu dùn tǔdòu** braised beef with
   potatoes; *g* **píjiǔ jī** stewed chicken
   in beer; *h* **kǎo yáng tuǐ** roast lamb
   leg; *i* **yějūn shāo dòufu** braised tofu
   with mushrooms; *j* **dòufu shāo yú**
   fried fish with tofu; *k* **shāguō yútóu**
   casseroled fish head; *l* **zhūròu dùn
   fěntiáo** braised pork with noodles;
   m **gān guō jī** griddle cooked chicken
   with pepper; *n* **xīhú cù yú** west lake
   fish in vinegar; *o* **shuàn yángròu**
   Mongolian lamb hotpot.

grammar

G1 Basic word order follows the English pattern: subject + verb + object:

> **Wǒ hē chá.** *I drink tea.*
> **Lǐ Wěi jiāo zhōngwén.** *Lǐ Wěi teaches Chinese.*

However,
- phrases referring to time and place generally go before the verb:
  Tā <u>měi tiān</u> jiāo Zhōngwén. *He teaches Chinese <u>every day</u>.*
  Tā <u>zài xiǎoxué</u> jiāo Zhōngwén. *He teaches Chinese <u>at primary school</u>.*

- the largest unit of time and place goes first:
  dates: **èrlínglíngbā nián** *2008* **bāyuè** *August* **èrshí'èr hào** *22nd*
  xīngqīwǔ *Friday*
  addresses: **Jiāngsū 215227 Wújiāng, Zhāng Huà Lù 453** *453 Zhang Hua Road, Wujiang, 215227 Jiangsu*

- question words reflect the position of the answer (see G10):
  Shìchǎng zài nǎr? *Lit. Market is where?*
  Nǐ hē shénme? *Lit. You drink what?*

G2 Nouns (words for people, things, places etc.) don't have a plural form, and rely on the context to make the meaning clear:

Wǒde péngyou Xǔ Qīng. *My friend Xǔ Qīng.*
Wǒ yǒu hěnduō péngyou. *I have many friends.*

- Chinese has no words for *the*. *A/an* is sometimes represented with **yī** + measure word.

G3 Personal pronouns (*I, she, us, they, etc.*) are the same in Chinese whether they're the subject or the object of a sentence.

wǒ	*I, me*	**wǒmen**	*we, us*
nǐ/nín	*you*	**nǐmen**	*you (more than one person)*
tā	*he/she, him/her*	**tāmen**	*they, them*
Wǒ ài nǐ.	*I love you.*	**Nǐ ài wǒ.**	*You love me.*

- **nín** is more formal than **nǐ** and is often used to address customers in shops or restaurants, and to show respect towards elderly people or senior people in business.

G4 Possession is indicated with **de**:

Xuán de chē *Xuán's car*
gōngsī de zǒngbù *the company('s) headquarters*
Shànghǎi de huǒchē *the Shanghai train*
wǒde gōngyù *my flat*

- **de** can be omitted when there's a close personal connection:
  wǒ māma, wǒde māma *my mother*
  nǐ jiā, nǐde jiā *your home*

- **wǒde, nǐde, tāde, wǒmende, nǐmende** and **tāmende** can mean both
  my and *mine, your* and *yours,* etc.
  Zhè shì tāde gōngyù. *This is his/her flat.* **Zhè shì wǒde.** *This is mine.*

G5 With a noun, **adjectives** of one syllable are used as in English:

xiǎo gōngyù *small flat*   **dà fángzi** *big house*

But when a description involves more than one syllable or an adverb, **de**
is added:

xiàndài de gōngyù *modern flat*   **hěn dà de fángzi** *very big house*

- **De** added to an adjective without a noun means *one(s)*:
  xiǎo de *the small one(s);* **dà de** *the big one(s);* **hóng de** *the red one(s).*

- **Tài** + adjective + **le** means *too* or *extremely*:
  tài guì le *too expensive;* **tài xiǎo le** *tiny*

- **Shì** *to be* is not used with adjectives:
  Gōngyù tǐng xiǎo. *The flat (is) rather small.*
  Fángzi hěn lǎo. *The house (is) very old.*
  Nǐ lèi/máng ma? *(Are) you tired/busy?*
  Wǒ bú lèi. *I (am) not tired.* **Tā tǐng máng.** *He (is) rather busy.*

This does not apply to describing nationality because, e.g. **Zhōngguórén**
means *a Chinese person.*

G6 The **preposition zài** can mean *to/in/at*:

Wǒ zhù zài Běijīng. *I live in Beijing.*
Wǒ zài fēijīchǎng gōngzuò. *I work at the airport.*

Zài also translates *to be in/at/on* without the need for *shì*:

Fēijīchǎng zài Pǔdōng. *The airport is in Pudong.*
Diàntī zài zuǒ biān. *The lift is on the left.*

(Quite unrelated to the above, **zài** before a verb means that someone's in the process of doing something: **Tā zài dú.** *She's reading right now.*)

G7 Numbers and measure words
Numbers are set out on pages 19 and 26.

- In lists of numbers, 1 is pronounced **yāo**, not **yī**.
- **Liǎng** is used instead of **èr** when talking about 2 of something.
- **Bǎifēnzhī** *percent* goes before the number: **bǎifēnzhī wǔshí** *50%*.
- Putting **dì** before a number turns it into an ordinal: e.g. **dì yī** *1st*, **dì èr** *2nd*, **dì sān** *3rd,* **dì shí** *10th,* **dì èrshíwǔ** *25th*.

G8 A noun cannot come directly after a number or **nà/zhè** *that/this*. A measure word (MW) has to come between them, and this categorises the noun that follows.

There are around 50 MWs, the most common being **ge**, used for people – **sān ge péngyou** *3 friends* – and also as the default option for things that don't fall within other categories, e.g. **bā ge yuè** *8 months*.

Some MWs equate to English concepts:
zhè bēi kāfēi *this cup of coffee*
liǎng píng shuǐ *2 bottles of water*
nà guàn píjiǔ *that can of beer*
sān bāo miàntiáo *3 packets of noodles*

Others have no equivalent and are not translated, e.g.
books: **zhè běn cídiǎn** *this dictionary*
vehicles: **liǎng liàng chē** *2 cars*
organisations: **nà jiā cānguǎn** *that restaurant*
light items of clothing: **liǎng tiáo lǐngdài** *2 ties*
large animals: **yī tóu dà xióngmāo** *1 panda*
flat paper items: **sān zhāng piào** *3 tickets*
small things: **nà zhī jī** *that chicken*
huge things: **nà zuò shān** *that mountain*

- MWs are also used with ordinal numbers: **dì wǔ běn shū** *the 5th book*. However, they're not used with **tiān** *day* and **nián** *year*, or with units of measurement, e.g. **jīn** *500g*, **gōnglǐ** *km*.

G9 Verbs (words like *to be*, *to live*, *to play*, *to understand*, *to have*, which refer to doing and being) have only one form regardless of who the subject is: **wǒ qù** *I go*; **wǒmen qù** *we go*; **tā qù** *he/she goes*.

- Even when there are two verbs together, there is only the one form:
  wǒ xiǎng qù/wǒ yào qù *I want to go*
  wǒ děi qù *I have to go*
  wǒ néng qù *I can go/I'm capable of going*
  wǒ kěyǐ qù *I can go/I'm allowed to go*
  wǒ huì yóuyǒng *I can swim/I know how to swim*
  wǒ xǐhuan yóuyǒng *I like to swim/swimming*

- To make a sentence negative in the present tense, you put bù before the verb: **wǒ bú qù** I don't go/I'm not going; **wǒ bú huì yóuyǒng** I can't swim. The only exception is **yǒu** have, there is/are which becomes **méi yǒu**.

- Repeating a verb introduces a casual note:
  Wǒ lái jièshao jièshao ... *Let me introduce* ...
  Wǒmen shuōshuo. *We'll have a word.*
  Tā xiǎngxiang. *She's thinking it over.*

G10 Questions

- Questions words such as **shénme** *what*, **shéi** *who*, **nǎ** *which*, **nǎr** (or **nǎli**) *where*, **shénme shíhou** *when*, **zěnme** *how* go in the same position as the answer will be:
  Nǐ hē shénme? *You drink what?* **Wǒ hē shuǐ.** *I drink water.*
  Cèsuǒ zài nǎr? *Toilet is where?* **Cèsuǒ zài lóuxià.** *Toilet is downstairs.*
  Nǐ shénme shíhou qù Běijīng? *You when go Beijing?*
  Wǒ míngtiān qù Běijīng. *I tomorrow go Beijing.*

- There are two ways of asking Yes/No questions:

  1 adding **ma** to the end of a statement:
    Tā shì lǎoshī. *He is a teacher.* **Tā shì lǎoshī ma?** *Is he a teacher?*
    Nǐ hē chá. *You drink tea.* **Nǐ hē chá ma?** *Do you drink tea?*

  2 repeating the verb or adjective, adding **bù** in the middle:
    Tā shì bú shì lǎoshī? *Is he a teacher?*
    Nǐ hē bù hē chá? *Do you drink tea?*
    Yángròu là bú là? *Is the lamb spicy?*

The only exception is **yǒu**, which adds **méi**:
Yǒu méi yǒu cānguǎn? *Is there a restaurant?*

- In questions offering alternatives, *or* is **háishi**. **Ma** is not added.
  Nǐ yào chá háishi kāfēi? *Would you like tea or coffee?*

G11 Answers

There's no catch-all translation for *yes* and *no*. Generally the verb or the adjective of the question is used in the answer:

Nǐ shì lǎoshī ma? *Are you a teacher?* **Shì** *Yes*; **Bú shì** *No*
Nǐmen hē bù hē kāfēi? *Do you drink coffee?* **Hē** *Yes*; **Bù hē** *No*
Nǐ zhīdào dìzhǐ ma? *Do you know the address?* **Zhīdào** *Yes*; **Bù zhīdào** *No*
Nǐ xǐhuan hǎixiān ma? *Do you like seafood?* **Xǐhuan** *Yes*; **Bù xǐhuan** *No*
Tā huì bú huì yóuyǒng? *Can he swim?* **Huì** *Yes*; **Bú huì** *No*
Nǐ lèi ma? *Are you tired.* **Hěn lèi** *Yes, very*; **Bú lèi** *No*
Tāmen yǒu piào ma? *Do they have tickets?* **Yǒu** *Yes*; **Méi yǒu** *No*

- **De** can be added to **shì** for emphasis:
  Nǐ shì Chang ma? *Are you Chang?* **Shì, shìde.** *Yes, yes I am.*

G12 Le, which has no direct equivalent in English, has many functions, including the following.

- With **tài** and an adjective it means *extremely* or *too*:
  tài dà le *extremely/too big*.

- At the end of a sentence, it indicates that a situation has changed:
  Wǒ líhūn le. *I'm divorced.*
  Wǒ méi yǒu qián le *I've no money (left)*.

- After a verb, it shows that the action occurred in the past:
  Wǒ qù le Zhōngguó. *I went to China/ I've been to China.*
  Tā mǎi le yī liàng chē *He bought a car.*
  Chī le ma? *Have you eaten? (often used as a greeting)*

Chinese–English glossary

A

Ài'ěrlán Ireland
àiren spouse, partner
Àodàlìyà Australia
Àodàlìyàrén Australian

B

ba *word used to make suggestions*
bā eight
bàba father
bǎi hundred
bài worship
báicài Chinese leaves
bǎihuò shāngdiàn department store
báilándì brandy
bái (mǐ)fàn boiled (lit. white) rice
bái pútáojiǔ white wine
bái(sè) white
bàn half
bàngōngshì office
bāngzhù help
bāo packet; include
bǎoxiǎnxiāng safe (box)
bāozi steamed bun
bāshí eighty
bāshíqī eighty seven
bēi glass, cup
běi north
Běijīngrén Beijing person
běn *measure word*
běndìrén local person
biān side
biàn *measure word*
biǎo form
biéde other
bīng ice
bīnguǎn hotel
bǐsà bǐng pizza
bōcài spinach
bōluó pineapple
bówùguǎn museum

bù not
bú kèqi you're welcome
bú xiè you're welcome

C

cài dish
càidān menu
cānguǎn restaurant
céng floor, level
cèsuǒ toilet
chá tea
chà yī kè a quarter to
Chángchéng the Great Wall
chǎo stir fry; noisy
chǎofàn fried rice
chāojí super
chāojí shìchǎng supermarket
chǎomiàn fried noodles
chāzi fork
chē car, vehicle
chéng city
chéngzi orange
chènshān shirt
chēzhàn bus stop
chī eat
chībǎo to be full
chīsù vegetarian
chuāncài Sichuan cuisine
chúnmáo pure wool
chūzūchē taxi
cì *measure word, number of train*
cōng onion
cóng from

D

dà big
dà hào large size
dài with
dàn egg
dānchéng single journey
dānjiān single room

dānrén fángjiān single room
dānshēn single (unmarried)
dànshì but
dāngrán of course
dào arrive
dǎoyóu tour guide
dàxiā prawn
dàxué university
de *word to show possession or to link up a long adjective with a noun*
Déguó Germany
Déguórén German (nationality)
děng wait
Déwén German (language)
dì *prefix in front of a number to make it an ordinal number*
diǎn o'clock
diǎncài order a meal
diànhuà telephone
diànhuà hàomǎ phone number
diàntī lift, escalator
dìdi younger brother
dìtiě underground
dìtú map
dōng east
dǒng understand
dònglì chēzǔ high-speed trains
dōu all, both
dòufu beancurd
dòuyá beansprout
duì corrrect
duìbuqǐ sorry
duìmiàn opposite
dùjià on holiday
duō many
duōdà how old

duō jiǔ how long
duōshao how many, how much

E

é goose
è hungry
èr two
ěrhuán earring
èrshí 20
èryuè February
érzi son

F

Fǎguó France
Fǎguórén French person
fàn rice, meal
fàncài food
fàndiàn restaurant, hotel
fángjiān room
fángshàiyóu suncream
Fǎwén French (language)
Fǎyǔ French (language)
fēicháng very, extremely
Fēilǜbīn The Phillipines
fēn *Chinese currency unit*
fēng wind
fēngshuǐ fengshui (lit. wind and water)
fēngzheng kite
fēnzhōng minute
fù pay
fùjìn nearby
fúwùyuán waiter, waitress
fúzhuāng clothes

G

gālí curry
gān bēi Cheers!
gāoxìng happy
ge *measure word*
gēge elder brother
gěi give; for
gēn with; follow
gèng even, more
gōngchǎng factory
gōngchéngshī engineer

gōngfu martial art
gōnggòng public
gōnggòng qìchē bus
gōnglǐ kilometre
gōngsī company
gōngyì měishù diàn arts and crafts shop
gōngyù flat, apartment
gōngyuán park
gōngzuò work, job
gòu enough
gòuwù zhōngxīn shopping centre
guǎi turn
guàn can, tin
guānglín be present
Guǎngzhōurén Guangzhou person
guānmén close
Gùgōng the Forbidden City
guì expensive
guìxìng surname
guó country
guójí nationality
guójiā country
guǒrén nut

H

hái still, in addition
hǎi sea
hǎibiān seaside
háishi or
hǎixiān seafood
háizi child
hán contain, include
hànbǎo bāo hamburger
Hánguó South Korea
Hánguórén Korean (nationality)
hǎo good, well
hào date, number, size
hǎochī delicious (for food)
hǎohē delicious (for drink)
háohuá luxury
hàomǎ number

hē drink
hé and, river
hēi(sè) black
hěn very
hěnduō many
hóng chá black tea
hónglǜdēng traffic light
hóng pútáojiǔ red wine
hóng(sè) red
hóngshāo stewed in dark soy sauce
hòu thick
hòulái late
hú lake
huā chá jasmine tea
huàláng art gallery
huānyíng welcome
huānyíng guānglín welcome
huáng(sè) yellow
huāyuán garden
huí jiàn see you later
huì can, able to
hùliánwǎng Internet
huǒchē train
huǒchēzhàn train station
huòzhě or
hùzhào passport

J

jī chicken
jīdàn egg
jī(ròu) chicken meat
jiā family
jiā dà extra large
jiān *measure word*; fried
jiàn *measure word*; to meet
Jiānádàrén Canadian
jiànshēnfáng gym
jiāo teach
jiāo *Chinese currency unit*
jiào call, be called
jiāoqū suburb
jiàoxǐng wake up
jiǎozi dumpling
jiārén family member
jiātíng family

jiéhūn married
jiějie elder sister
jiēkǒu connection point
jièlán Chinese broccoli
jièshào introduce
jiézhàng to settle the bill
jǐhào what number, what date
jīn *Chinese weight unit, equal to half a kilo*
jìn enter
jīntiān today
jīnglǐ manager
jīnwǎn tonight
jǐ suì how old
jiǔ wine
jiǔbā wine bar
jiǔdiàn hotel
jiǔshí 90
jiǔyuè September
jìzhě journalist
jú bureau
júhuā chá chrysanthemum tea
jùyuàn opera house
júzi tangerine
júzi zhī orange juice

K
kǎbùqínuò cappuccino
kāfēi coffee
kāfēiguǎn café
kāi open
kāimén open
kànkan to have a look
Kānpéilā Canberra
kǎo roasted
kǎoyā roast duck
kělè cola
kěyǐ can, may
kòng vacant
kōngtiáo air-conditioning
kuài *Chinese currency unit*
kuàijìshī accountant
kuàizi chopsticks

kuàngquán shuǐ mineral water

L
là spicy hot
lái come
lán(sè) blue
Lánkǎisītè Lancaster
lǎoshī teacher
le *grammatical partical*
lǐ *unit of length, 1 li = 0.5 kilometre*
liàng *measure word*
liǎng two
liǎngrén fángjiān twin room
líhūn divorce
líng zero
lǐngdài tie
liú leave
liù 6
liùshí 60
lìzhī lychee
lízi pear
lóngxiā lobster
lóushàng upstairs
lóuxià downstairs
lù road, route
lǔcài Shandong cuisine
lǜ chá green tea
lùkǒu crossroad
Lúndūn London
lǜ(sè) green
lǔshuǐ marine sauce, gravy
lǜshī lawyer
lǚxíngshè travel agent
lǚyóu travel, tour
lǚyóujú tourist board

M
ma *question word*
mǎi buy
mài sell
májiàng marjong
Mǎláixīyà Malaysia
māma mother
mǎmǎhūhū so-so

mǎn full
màn slow
mángguǒ mango
mànmàn chī enjoy your meal
máo *Chinese currency unit*
màozi hat, cap
Měiguó America
Měiguórén American (person)
mèimei younger sister
měi tiān everyday
méi yǒu do not have
miàn(tiáo) noodles
mǐfàn rice
mì guā melon
mǐjiǔ rice wine
mí lù to be lost
mǐncài Fujian cuisine
míngpiàn name/business card
míngtiān tomorrow
míngxìnpiàn postcard
míngzi name
mínzú minority nationality
mógu mushroom
mótuōchē motorbike
mùdìdì destination

N
nǎ which
nà that, there
nàbiān over there
nǎ guó rén? what nationality are you?
nǎi chá tea with milk
nǎinai grandmother (on father's side)
nǎli where
nǎli nǎli not at all
nàme then, in that case
nán south; male
Nánjīngrén Nanjing person
nán péngyou boyfriend
nǎr where

ne *grammatical particle*
néng to be able to, can
nǐ you
nián year
nǐde your, yours
nǐ hǎo hello
nǐmen you (plural)
nín you (formal)
nín hǎo hello (formal)
níngméng lemon
niúliú sliced beef
niúnǎi milk
niúròu beef
Niǔyuē New York
nóngcūn countryside
nǚ female
nǚ'ér daughter
nǚ péngyou girlfriend
nǚshì madam

P

páigǔ spare ribs
pángbiān next to
péngyou friend
piányi cheap
piào ticket
piàoliang beautiful
pígé leather
pījiān pashmina, shawl
píjiǔ beer
píng bottle
píngguǒ apple
pǔkuài lièchē fast ordinary train
pútáojiǔ wine
pǔtōng lièchē ordinary train

Q

qī 7
qiān thousand
qián money
qiǎokèlì chocolate
qìchē automobile
qǐng invite; please
qīngcài green vegetables
qǐngkè to treat somebody (to a meal)

qīngnián lǚshè youth hostel
qǐng wèn may I ask?
qīngzhēng steamed
qīshí 70
qítā other
qù to go

R

ràng to allow
rén person
Rénmínbì (RMB) *Chinese currency*
rènshi to get to know a person
Rìběn Japan
Rìběnrén Japanese (person)
Rìwén Japanese (language)
Rìyǔ Japanese (language)
ròu meat
ruǎnwò soft sleeper
ruǎnzuò soft seat

S

sān 3
sānshí 30
shān mountain
shāngdiàn shop
Shànghǎirén Shanghai people
shàngwǔ morning
shàngyī jacket
shānshuǐhuà landscape painting
shǎo little, few
shāo děng just a minute
sháozi spoon
shēng to be born
shěng province
shénme what
shénme shíhou when
shí 10
shì to be; city; try
shícài seasonal vegetable
shìchǎng market
shìde yes

shí'èryuè December
shíhou time
shìshi to have a try, try on
shíyīyuè November
shì zhōngxīn town centre
shǒujī mobile phone
shòupiàochù ticket office
shǒutíbāo handbag
shuāngrén fángjiān double room
shuǐ water
shuǐguǒ diàn greengrocer's
shuō speak, say
sī silk
sǐ to die, death
sì 4
sìshí 40
sù vegetarian
suàn garlic
suānlà hot and sour
sùcài vegetarian dish
Sūgélán Scotland
Sūgélánrén Scottish (person)
suì years old
suìshu years old (used when asking old people their age)

T

tā he/she/him/her
tài too, extremely
Tàiguó Tailand
tàijí t'ai chi
tàitai wife, Mrs
tāmen they/them
tāmende their/theirs
tāng soup
táng sugar
tángcù sweet and sour
táocí porcelain
táozi peach
tèkuài lièchē express fast trains
tiān day

tóngshì colleague, workmate

túshūguǎn library

W

wàigōng grandfather (on mother's side)

wàipó grandmother (on mother's side)

wàn 10,000

wǎn evening, night

wǎn'ān goodnight

wǎng towards

wǎngbā internet café

wǎngfǎn return journey

wǎnshang evening

wǎnshang hǎo good evening

wèi measure word; hello on the phone

Wēi'ěrshì Wales

Wēi'ěrshìrén Welsh (person)

wéijīn scarf

wēishìjì whisky

wō nest

wǒ I, me

wò lie

wǒde my, mine

wǒmen we, us

wū house

wǔ 5

wūlóng chá oolong tea

wǔshí 50

X

xī west

xiā shrimp

xià next

xiànchāo jī cash machine

xiǎng want, think about

xiāngbīn champagne

xiāngcài Hunan cuisine

Xiānggǎng Hong Kong

Xiānggǎngrén Hong Kong person

xiāngjiāo banana

xiàngliàn necklace

xiānsheng sir, Mr

xiànzài now

xiǎo small, young

xiǎojie Miss

xiǎomàibù corner shop

xiǎoshí hour

xiàwǔ afternoon

xià yī tàng next train or bus

Xībānyá Spain

Xībānyáwén Spanish (language)

Xībānyáyǔ Spanish (language)

xībiān West

xīcānguǎn Western food restaurant

xièxie thank, thank you

xī guā watermelon

xīhóngshì tomato

xǐhuan like

xìng surname

xīngjí star grade

xíngli luggage

xīngqī week

xīngqī'èr Tuesday

xīngqīliù Saturday

xīngqīsān Wednesday

xīngqīsì Thursday

xīngqītiān Sunday

xīngqīwǔ Friday

xīngqīyī Monday

Xīní Sydney

Xīnjiāpō Singapore

Xīnxīlánrén New Zealander

xìnyòngkǎ credit card

xǐyīfáng laudrette

xué to learn, to study

xuésheng student

xuéyuàn college

Y

yā duck

yángróng thick pure wool

yángròu lamb

yángtáo starfruit

yánsè colour

yāo one

yào to want, need

yàoshi key

yě also

yéye grandfather (on father's side)

yēzi coconut

yī one

yī bǎi 100

yībiàn once

Yìdàlìrén Italian (person)

Yìdàlìwén Italian (language)

yìdiǎn a little bit

yīgòng altogether

Yíhéyuán the Summer Palace

yī kè a quarter, 15 minutes

yí lù píng ān bon voyage

Yìndùníxīyà Indonesia

Yīnggélán UK

Yīnggélánrén British (person)

Yīngguórén British (person)

yīngtáo cherry

Yīngwén English (language)

Yīngyǔ English (language)

yìngwò hard sleeper

yìngzuò hard seat

yínháng bank

yīnyuètīng music hall

yīshēng doctor

yíxià a little (used after a verb)

yīyàng the same

yīyuàn hospital

yīyuè January

yìzhí straight, along

yòng use

Yōnghégōng Yonghe Palace (a Tibetan Buddhist temple)

yǒu to have; right

yòu again
yóujú post office
yóumèn braised
yóupiào stamp
yóuyǒngchí swimming
pool
yú fish
yǔ rain
yù jade
yuán *unit of currency*
yuǎn far
yùdìng to reserve
yuè month
yuècài Cantonese cuisine
Yuènán Vietnam
yùshì bathroom

Z

zài in, on, at; again
zàijiàn goodbye
zǎocān breakfast
zǎoshang morning
zǎoshang hǎo good
morning
zěnme how
zěnmeyàng how; how
about it?; how are you?
zhá deep fried
zhāng *measure word*
zhàngdān bill
zhàngfu husband
zhǎnlǎnhuì exhibition
zhànpiào standing
(ticket)
zhǎo look for, find
zhāodàisuǒ economy
guest houses
zhàopiàn photo
zhè this
zhècài Zhejiang cuisine
zhēn really; real, true
zhēnsī pure silk
zhēnzhū pearl
zhèr here
zhèxiē these
zhǐ only
zhídá tèkuài express
trains

zhīdao know
zhídào until
zhíyè profession
zhōng middle
Zhōngcān Chinese
cuisine
Zhōngguó China
Zhōngguórén Chinese
(person)
Zhōngguó Tiělù China
Rail
Zhōngwén Chinese
(language)
zhōngxīn centre
zhōu provincial capital
zhōumò weekend
zhù live, stay
zhǔcài main course
zhǔrèn director
zhūròu pork
zhǔshí staple
carbohydrate
zhǔxí chairperson
zhǔyi idea
zìxíngchē bicycle
zǒu walk
zǒulù walk, on foot
zuìdī jià lowest price
zuìjìn recently; nearest
zuò sit, do
zuǒ left
zuǒ biān left side